Once you start reading Jan Coleman's book, you won't want to stop. She will touch your heart and encourage your spirit with honesty and a call to holiness, yet lavish you with humor. If your spirit is sagging because of the locusts nibbling at your peace, start reading! You will find immediate hope and help!

—Kathy Collard Miller
author, *Why Do I Put So Much Pressure on Myself?*

One of the most bitingly honest books I've ever had the pleasure of reading. With the boldness of a prophet and the graciousness of a heart full of mercy, Jan has woven together stories of devastation and restoration. Like a good novel, you won't want to put this book down. As a powerful teaching, you will be moved to a higher calling to intimacy with God.

—Eva Marie Everson,
author, *Shadow of Dreams*

Gutsy. Transparent. Real. Honest, powerful, not sugar coated but true-life stories of ordinary women whose lives were once tripped bare by the locusts, but are now a living testimony to God's glorious restoration plan. Jan also teaches us about one of the minor prophets you never hear much about—Joel. I highly recommend this well-written book.

—Laura Jensen Walker
author, *Thanks for the Mammogram!*
and *Ferris Wheels, Daffodils, & Hot Fudge Sundaes*

Jan blends Old Testament teaching with the lives of women who've not only survived loss and disappointment, but thrived in spite of them to be better than before. I know. I've been there.

—Florence Littauer
author, *Personality Plus*
Founder of CLASS Speakers, Inc.

If your journey has led to relationship troubles, financial battles, physical limitations, the painful consequences of misguided decisions, or any other "locust lesson" beyond your control, God is waiting to help you turn your life around. *After the Locusts* is filled with biblically sound direction to help you get back on course.

—Allison Gappa Bottke
author, compiler, *God Allows U-Turns* series

When it seems you've been stripped of your joy by life's hardships, it's hard to put one faithful foot in front of the other. *After the Locusts* is a book that will givse you encouragement, tangible help, and hope. Its strong teaching and Jan's warm vulnerability will help you rest in God's arms as you rebuild your life.

—Janet Holm McHenry
author, *PrayerWalk* and *Girlfriend Gatherings*

Jan reminds us that, despite life's losses, God is in control. If you long for hope and victory over despair, you will find it in these pages.

—Linda Evans Shepherd
coauthor, *Share Jesus Without Fear*
radio host, *Right to the Heart*

No platitudes. No easy answers. No spiritual Band-Aids that don't stick. This book captures the truths of God's promises. Sudden grief, lost relationships, abuse, and rejection are never beyond the reach of the Lord's loving power of restoration. Jan realistically and graphically portrays the struggle to trust the Lord when bad things happen. This book stirs up courage, anticipation, and hope to allow God to transform tradgedy and disappointment into overwhelming victory and joy.

—Mike Petrillo
Marriage and Family Therapist
Executive Director, Christian Encounter Ministries

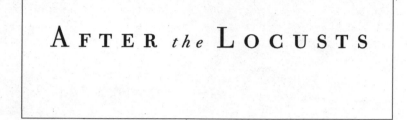

AFTER *the* LOCUSTS

0–8054–2490–3
Published by Broadman & Holman Publishers,
Nashville, Tennessee

Dewey Decimal Classification: 248
Subject Heading: CHRISTIAN LIVING

Library of Congress Cataloging-in-Publication Data

Coleman, Jan, 1948–
   After the locusts : restoring ruined dreams, reclaiming wasted years / Jan
   Coleman.
      p. cm.
   Includes bibliographical references (p.).
   ISBN 0–8054–2490–3 (pb.)
   1. Women—Religious life. 2. Loss (Psychology)—Religious aspects—
   Christianity. I. Title.

BV4527 .C63 2002
248.8'43—dc21
                                                              2001049931
         1 2 3 4 5 6 7 8 9 10 06 05 04 03 02

AFTER *the* LOCUSTS

JAN COLEMAN

RESTORING RUINED DREAMS, RECLAIMING WASTED YEARS

BROADMAN
& HOLMAN
PUBLISHERS

NASHVILLE, TENNESSEE

CONTENTS

PREFACE

SOMEONE ONCE SAID that joy and sorrow are inseparable. The deeper sorrow carves into your being, the more joy you can absorb.

I wouldn't have believed it twenty years ago. Not when the locusts of despair swooped into my life and ruined my dreams. But now, *after the locusts,* there is a deep valley in my soul—not a dark valley but a hollow crevice for joy to settle in. Joy I could never have known without the storm.

Hannah Hurnard defines joy as "sorrow accepted and transformed," and I know it's true.

Ten years ago a shattered woman came to our weekly women's prayer breakfast, searching for hope. Because I had been like her—empty, confused, and hurting—I volunteered to mentor Ginger through her crisis time. Right away I shared God's promise from Joel 2:25, "I will repay you for the years the locusts have eaten." In the King James Version it reads: "I will restore to you the years."

In my painful yesterdays someone gave me that promise, and I clung to it. I watched God not only repay me for the years but mold my life into something better and richer than ever before. If she allowed Him, God would do the same for Ginger.

Do you know the word *comfort* comes from the Latin word *fortis,* which means "strong"? As God comforts through loss, we are built up, through our resources, our new challenges, and our deeper faith.

After Ginger I met dozens of women who needed their spirits lifted in dark times, and as I shared Joel 2:25, many found comfort and hope. Some opted to decline the challenge, wishing that God would wave His magic wand and heal them. Instead they chose their own way. As a result, some ended up right back where they started, facing emptiness and despair.

Nobody urged me to write this book, but the idea kept tickling my brain, and when I brought the concept to a writers' conference in 1989, an editor said, "Unique idea—send me some chapters."

I went home to my computer and bit my fingernails. A good idea is one thing; executing it is another. As I sat staring at an empty screen, it became clear that I wasn't ready to revisit my own pain and loss yet.

Then last year the notion came on again, and this time with a fervor. *Remember Ginger? Start with her story. Bring it alive on the page. Write that locust book!* By this time I felt ready. *But, Lord, I need so many stories of ruined dreams, wasted years. Where do I find them?*

The answer came clearly. *Look around. You know who they are. They've come through your life in the last ten years.*

The vignettes you'll read on the following pages are mostly women whose stories I know well, and each has not only survived loss and regret but also has answered the challenge to work closely with God in the process. Each woman has found new purpose and sufficiency, and each agreed she wouldn't have missed the *lesson from the locusts* for anything.

> I walked a mile with Pleasure
> She chatted all the way;
> And left me none the wiser
> For all she had to say.
> I walked a mile with Sorrow
> A never a word said she;
> But, oh, the things I learned from her
> When Sorrow walked with me.
> —*Robert Browning Hamilton*

A WORD OF THANKS

To every woman who gave me access to her heart and unique story: You shared less about your loss than about God's personally designed repayment plan. Thank you for your gutsy honesty. There is nothing more powerful, more life-changing, than the truth.

And to Ginger for opening your life to me the moment we met. You allowed me an orchestra seat for the greatest show on earth—seeing God restore the years the locusts have eaten. Your transparency taught me so much.

To Broadman & Holman and Len Goss, I'm honored that you believed in the message of the locusts and chose to publish my book.

A few select "reader" friends had helpful comments, most of which made the book much better. Thanks to my friend, Laura, and my grade-school classmate, Roanne. You pored over the text for typos, awkward words and phrases. (No, I don't mind your being so picky.)

To my daughters, Jennifer and Amy, whose young lives were ravaged by locusts. I admire your courage in letting me tell all and use your real names. I'm proud of how you've turned your lives around.

To Carl, whose gentle encouragement kept me going with this project. You're truly my partner.

To my prayer breakfast pals and Monday night Bible study partners, I'm glad for the times we shared our souls. Together we learned to pray, not for easier lives, but to be stronger, more faithful women.

INTRODUCTION

I NEVER SET OUT to get cozy with Joel. He's a rather dim figure among the minor prophets of the Bible, and we hardly hear much about him. But knowing this guy changed my life. His name, a common one in Israel, means "the Lord is God."

You've got to love a guy with a name like that.

Joel's book, wedged between the books of Hosea and Amos, is thought to take place eight hundred years before Christine. It deals with a locust plague, not such a big deal considering bug blitzes were quite common in those days. But this one was unique. A complete disaster, it wiped out everything. The locusts came in successive swarms, each destroying what the others had left behind.

But God had a purpose, to use the plague to stir the people into a new sense of Himself.

Thus, along comes Joel. With vivid word pictures and powerful emotions, he pleads to the people of Israel to get the message; there are dark days ahead, yes, but God desires to bless His people who live honorably in the face of struggle and loss.

What does He want? Nothing, just your whole heart—that's it.

That's it? Seems simple enough, doesn't it? But not when your heart is bruised and weary. Not when your world is upside down in chaos.

Trusting God isn't always easy.

It took me a bit of time to piece this truth together. Though I had the promise of Joel 2:25 tacked on my refrigerator, I took some foolish turns on my way to healing. You'll hear about them all as you read this book.

God didn't need to send out great armies to bring people to their knees in total dependence on Him in order to stress that He was in control of everything. Or to show His kindness, His every intention of showering them with good gifts after their loss.

All He needed was a swarm of little insects.

I'm not a Bible scholar, but I've studied this man, Joel, and he wins the contest as my most popular prophet. Come and meet him, won't you? *After the Locusts* highlights women whose lives are a testimony to God's restoration plan, but it also takes you through a bit of the Old Testament with a straightforward, no-nonsense guy with great compassion for those who hurt.

You'll see after each chapter heading a Scripture verse from Joel that becomes the theme. Even though Joel's words apply to a specific event in Jewish history, there's a storehouse of hope in them for today.

This book may not answer all your questions or cover the exact difficulty you face, but I pray you'll be stirred to a new understanding of your loss. As you read honest accounts of women who've suffered, and not only survived but thrived, I think you'll be inspired.

As a bonus, you'll get to know Joel and the wonderful promise he offers from the Lord. So let's get going, OK?

CHAPTER ONE

THE BIG BUG BLITZ

Has anything like this ever happened in your days?
—Joel 1:2

THE LOCUSTS WERE AT IT AGAIN.

I knew it the moment I saw the clouded look in her eyes, by the trance-like way she kept pouring cream into her coffee. "I can't believe this is happening," the woman murmured and then stared out the frosty window to the restaurant parking lot.

Slipping into my designated chair at Sweet Pea's Cafe, I gave Ginger a weak nod. I hadn't been formally introduced yet, but I'd been briefed on the new gal who might be joining us for our weekly prayer breakfast. *She is going through a very rough time.* Ginger looked up slowly, clutching a napkin to her moist eyes. "I don't think I can go on. I feel so alone."

Arms enveloped her as she choked back the sobs. The horror-story gaze on her face revealed the rough time she faced. She had the look I knew so well, as if her insides were being ravaged by some alien creatures.

Paralysis of the heart. Attack on the soul.

While I quietly motioned to the waitress I'd like my usual poached egg on rye, Ginger's fist went to her lips. "Oh, I'm so embarrassed."

Together we pressed her to get it all out, share her story. We were a safe haven, all seasoned veterans of life's struggles, a group of women who had been meeting together every week for many years, praying, bringing hurts like this before the Lord.

My hunch turned out to be right; Ginger's dreams were shattered. Her husband of twenty-five years had suddenly left and this breakfast at Sweet Pea's was her first time out from behind the drawn blinds of her mountain home, except to go to church. With the pastor's urging to find someone who has been there, Ginger phoned Jeanne, who had taught her son in school years ago.

Could Jeanne have some remedy for this pain? The valium wasn't numbing it enough.

"Come to prayer breakfast," Jeanne encouraged her, then promptly left a message urging me not to make this one of the days I decided to sleep in. Jeanne is always scheming for the Lord.

Sitting across the table from Ginger, I observed a soft-spoken woman in her forties with ravishing hair the color of California poppies. My writer's mind envisioned her as a character from a gothic novel, an elegant Irish Lass, searching for a "happily ever after."

Ginger's would now be very much in doubt.

"How can we pray for you?" one of our gals asked.

"That he comes back," she pleaded. "Or that God takes me home. I feel like there's nothing left for me now."

Those words pricked my heart, and I began to pray silently: *Lord, help her to cling to your promise—that you will restore the years the locusts have eaten.*

Though we aren't dealing with the plagues of old, trials and misfortunes still invade our lives, and they still make unwelcome visits that test everything we've ever trusted. Plagues of the heart can come in many forms—divorce, thesudden death of a loved one, painful abuse, a ravaging illness, a miserable marriage, a personal failure that rocks our foundations. The stories are different, but the feelings of damage and wasted years, emptiness, and fear are common to us all.

Those thoughts darted through my mind as I glanced around our breakfast table that morning over eight years ago. We had our matriarch, a widow who had lost a precious son decades before and now faced blindness; three of us abandoned by our mates; one whose son still battled drugs in his forties; another whose daughter is lost to the homosexual lifestyle. And yet another, whose decision to leave her first husband thirty years ago had brought some painful consequences.

There we sat at our usual table, a collage of ruined dreams and wasted years, a hodgepodge of tender hurts that bound us together each Friday morning. There are few secrets in our group; rather, we lay bare our hearts, expecting to hear the ruthless truth from one another and be better for it. We laugh hysterically and often cry before the eggs and oatmeal raisin pancakes arrive, all the while deepening our faith in a loving God whom we trust has a purpose for it all.

Ginger had come to the right place.

After our time of prayer that morning, I took a final sip of my lemon tea and felt a friendly nudge under the table from Jeanne. I had no trouble interpreting the gesture: *She needs you. You've been through this.*

You can say that again.

Yes, I'd been there, standing in the field of ruined dreams. Without the man who said he'd love me forever, without the cherished family life I had planned for as a young girl. Everything destroyed and me all alone with two confused daughters. I remember trying to stop the gush of tears as I surveyed what was left of my life. I looked out at the dried-up ground, wondering—would anything grow there ever again?

Bob not only abandoned me, but his rejection also shattered my daughters and sent them rebelling through their teenage years, their innocence destroyed.

Yet God had done some amazing things in the aftermath, not only with me, but also with so many other women that came through my life.

While our table talk still focused on Ginger, my mind drifted to locusts. Can you picture them, Hollywood-style, when Charlton Heston, as Moses in *The Ten Commandments,* cast them as the eighth plague over Egypt? Well-deserved judgment for Pharoah's wickedness, don't you think? But not until years later, during an episode of *Little House on the Prairie,* did my emotions stir for the helpless victim of these killer insects. A pioneer woman, clutching to the porch rails, watched their descent into her life, a swarm so dense you couldn't see through the thick darkness. After they were gone, they left not a leaf—nothing but grayish-brown dust.

Good for nothing but to choke on.

Have you felt like that pioneer woman? After my loss I *was* her, staring from my sod house at the carefully tended fields being ransacked by zillions of icky bugs that came soaring out of nowhere. Every day they ascended in immense numbers so dense I couldn't see the sun through them.

They turned my day into night.

We're not talking about little crickets, not about harmless little creatures flitting through the garden. When the locusts paid me a personal call, they were out to destroy all I had toiled so hard for.

And they nearly did.

FEAST DAY

First came the *creeping* locust, whispering that this thing can't really be happening to me. It's a nightmare, just cover your head, don't tell anyone, just pretend everything will be fine tomorrow.

Then the *gnawing* locust, whittling away my confidence. If only you were a better woman, this wouldn't be happening to you. If only you had more faith, you wouldn't feel so empty right now.

Next the *stripping* locusts, exposing the hurt and anger. I hate him. I hate me. I hate God. I hate everyone who smiles at me.

Finally, the *swarming* locusts, stripping me completely bare, speeding me straight into a life of uncertainty. All those years of tilling, spading, planting a crop in neatly planned rows. Wasted years. *Now, look at you—how will you ever start over?*

Where was my prophet to plead on my behalf like so many did in the Old Testament? My prophet never showed up, but my calamity sure did. It came and dined and left me with a bill I was not equipped to pay. Beyond the pain a new experience waited for me, strange and frightening, the last thing I ever expected.

None of it made sense for many years, but through it, I found contentment in my situation. There are now new crops in my field, new dreams stored up in my barn.

They're God's dreams this time, instead of my own.

My heart ached that morning for Ginger, for the snuffing out of cherished dreams, for the medley of grief that plays on the soul when it's wounded, and for the fear that lurks over our shoulder when loss pays such an unwelcome visit.

Ginger needed assurance that her God is reliable, that He would see her through this, and that somehow He would help her clean up the impossible mess. Because I had been witness to the Lord's wonderful restoration plan, I had no doubts of this. Neither did our Friday morning ladies, because despite difficult circumstances that still lingered for some, they held on to solid evidence of a faithful God.

But Ginger needed more than a Friday morning fix. I could see that.

Suddenly, I began to squirm in my chair. *But, Lord, she needs a mentor, an encourager, a sister in sorrow. That's a big commitment! And you know I really don't want to revisit my*

own pain and loss again. Couldn't you have sent her to some-
one else? Don't you have some other task for me now? I'll
reconsider teaching Sunday school, maybe preschoolers?

Naturally, God paged me with an instant message.
Remember what you tossed in at the end of your prayer last
week? Use me, Lord. Make me a blessing.

Oh? This is one of your divine appointments? I see. Still, I
secretly hoped that Ginger's husband would magically return
in a few days to create a powerful testimony of love restored.
Either way, it would be a long, hard road, and she would need
a friend.

Ginger's sniffles broke my thoughts. "I gave him all the best
years of my life," she warbled. Silver-haired Betty squeezed her
shoulder. "There, there, sweetie. Now don't cry. Just remember, all things work together for good for those who love
God."

Forcing a smile, Ginger stiffened, brushing a strand of cop-
per hair behind one ear. She still clutched a few locks when I
beamed in on her distress signal. She didn't need Romans 8:28
right then. Later she would appreciate it, even relish in it, but
right then the last thing on her mind was rebuilding her life;
she was bleeding, in agony, protecting a gaping, open wound.
She had come to us hoping for first-aid provisions—a tourni-
quet, a sling, a good strong crutch.

Not to mention an antidote for stinging bug bites.

When I looked over at Ginger, pale and stone-faced, I made
up my mind to volunteer as her guide through this desert experience. My mission, should she accept the offer, would be to
show her how to welcome the difficulties that now poured into
her life.

Huh? Welcome the storm clouds? you might be wondering.
Welcome this plague I'm now facing?

You can't see me, but I'm nodding. Yes, that's exactly what
you can do.

Of course, no sane person sends out invitations to a bug banquet. We never ask for a swarm of trouble or disaster, but when it arrives, we can learn to welcome the experience. Oh, not warmly, the way you would welcome a friend, but wisely, like you might a visiting professor who is taking over the college course. You may think the guy's presentation stinks, but there are valuable lessons to learn if you don't ditch the class.

Perhaps you're battling locusts today. I have good news for you.

In the midst of my own battles, I found a great promise of hope tucked in the book of Joel, right in the second chapter. Though the prophet preached to ancient Judah, his message is for us today. And it is a powerful one.

This promise will reshape your life if you let it.

Stick around. You can't miss the message: See the Lord in this experience. Remain true to Him even though you may not understand what has happened to you. What you see in the end will be worth it.

It's no mistake this book has come into your life at this time. Maybe you've suffered a loss, or someone close to you has, and you're searching for ways to find or offer comfort.

As you travel through this book with Ginger, me, and a host of others, you'll see that no one escaped the devastation in the time of the prophet Joel. From priests to peasants, nobody was out of bounds of the disaster that came along.

Today few of us escape loss. It seems to be everywhere, in so many of our relationships and families. With it can come confusion and anger and questions for God. Maybe you're there now, in the midst of trouble, praying for a break in the dark clouds. Perhaps you've struggled with ruined dreams, shattered hopes, and discouragement.

You may be limping down a narrow, rocky road, cold and tired and bleeding from a broken heart. Everything you planted in hope and expectation has been swept away and along with it your trust in God's promises.

Perhaps you can relate to the feelings of the women in my Sunday school class. The first day we met I passed around a basket filled with collected items from around the house and asked each woman to take one and use it to describe something about herself. Horti took the meat tenderizer. "My husband killed himself a year and a half ago. I have no children, no family. I'm not wallowing, I'm just marinating in God's love right now."

Ginny held the miniature Coleman lantern flashlight. "I lost my husband to cancer last year. I need some light to find my way." A young single mother, who had suffered years of abuse, had a spool of yarn and burst into tears, "I'm hanging by a thread."

You might be blaming yourself for the years you wasted on disastrous choices. Feeling that you've failed yourself, you've failed God.

So what do you do?

Take heart. Even the steel-tempered Scarlett O'Hara could never have fought off the locusts if they had threatened her beloved Tara. The key is not to panic. Don't be tempted to sell those broken dreams for pennies on the dollar. Stand firm, dig in, and hold on to your barren fields. With God behind the plow with you, your life will produce again—and better than before.

God's promises are like stars—the darker the night,
the brighter they shine.

Years ago, that chilly December morning at Sweet Pea's, I made Ginger an offer she wouldn't refuse. *Hang in there girl. Stick out the siege. I'll be there with you.* As a bonus I would throw in a pair of old frayed boots to trudge through the dirt clods, my jumbo broom to beat at the bugs (it does absolutely no good, but the exercise makes you feel so much better), and a pledge from the Master Gardener.

His promise? To restore the ruined dreams and wasted years.

If you stick with us to the end of the book, you will know much of what God taught us. We'll help you work through the questions, show you how to endure the painful attack on your soul and not run away to something worse, and most of all—how to profit from the trials.

Our God is the ultimate conservationist. He won't let one groan or tear be wasted. He recycles them into fuel for our future; they're like a bottle of high-potency vitamins guaranteed to provide energy if we follow all the directions.

Only His aren't in small print.

And hear this: He wants to be involved in this whole restoring process as your partner. You will not be alone.

If you are looking for a formula-type solution for your situation, it's not in here. But what you will find are some gutsy accounts from women who've lived through the wasteland of death, disappointment, and sorrow. Through their stories you cannot help but embrace hope and trust.

Whatever your circumstances, I hope you'll grow stronger and more hopeful from Ginger's journey to a new life. You will also read stories of other women who've not only survived but also lived on in spite of their losses to find renewed meaning for their lives. Each woman highlighted in the following pages is more fulfilled and more fruitful for God now than she could ever have imagined before she faced her loss.

By the time you finish reading, I hope you'll have a clearer idea of how God intends to redeem the losses in your life. As an added bonus, you'll get to know the prophet Joel, and I think you'll come to like this "before and after" kind of guy. He paints a pretty dismal picture of the "before," but wait until you get a glimpse of the "after"!

Pretty good stuff.

As we follow Joel through two chapters, we meet one of the great realists in Bible history—a man who looked at things from the right perspective. And knowing him a bit better will help you go from the earthly view—I have lost those years—to the heavenly confidence that the years will be restored in a surprising and wonderful way.

Think about this. The locust plague in Joel was an experience beyond compare, something so astonishing that people would be talking about it for generations to come. They would be telling their children and grandchildren about the ruin "in the old days" and how the Lord turned it all around.

But, most important, they would tell them how it changed the hearts of the people.

Your dreams may be devastated, but know this to be true: the best is yet to come. I know the path you're trudging down right now is not much fun. Restoration projects are a lot of work; they take tremendous commitment for months, maybe years of sweat equity. But when you're over the hump, when you can look back and see the fruits of your labor, you'll consider it the most soul-stirring work of your life.

For now, pull up the straps on your overalls, and go find a good pitchfork. Let the replanting begin.

She that lives in hope plants a crop where there are few seeds.

CHAPTER TWO

JUST HOW LONG IS THIS DRY SPELL?

Tell it to your children,
and let your children tell it to their children,
and their children to the next generation.
—Joel 1:3

FROST SHIMMERED ON MY CAMELLIA BUDS like sugary cake icing as I watched Ginger park her car. She hesitated before walking up my front steps. From my kitchen window every fiber in me hoped that we would connect and that she would trust me.

It was right before Christmas, but it certainly wouldn't be much of a holiday for her now.

Before the doorbell rang, I thought of other women I had met over the years, women who fell or were pushed into difficulties that put them to the test of their strength and faith. I'd seen many trot off to seek relief in all the wrong places—a relationship, new lifestyle, pills, seclusion, denial. They simply dug in their heels and refused to venture very far down a road that seemed too rough.

This journey to restoration is not for the tenderfooted. Your shoes pinch, and your toes cramp. I'd watched many hobble right back where they started, facing a barren field.

Just like me. With that thought still floating, I answered Ginger's knock on the door. I prayed, *Please Lord, don't let*

Ginger make the same mistakes I did. She's so vulnerable and softhearted.

As I brewed a pot of my favorite cinnamon tea, she sat at my kitchen table and lamented, "I thought this only happened to other people. It's such a nightmare."

My agreeing nod said it all. Whatever the issue, there are no nightmares spookier than looking in the mirror and wondering, *Who am I now? Where do I go from here?*

When we're bushwhacked out of nowhere, we come up loaded with questions. Ginger wanted answers. *How could he have made plans to leave without me ever guessing? Was there another woman?* And she blamed herself. *Was this a failure on my part? What can I do to stop this, make him change his mind? What about an exotic vacation to recreate our romance? I could have a makeover, liposuction on my cottage-cheese thighs.*

Where did she go wrong?

Did God send this disaster as He did in the Old Testament, because of sin and rebellion in her life? Did He deliver a heartache just to punish her somehow?

I had tormented myself with those questions too.

It's complicated, but I finally resolved that no matter what happened, God loved me. He didn't ordain me to suffer the pain of a disastrous marriage merely to shape me up.

I don't think He had planned for me to marry a man whose cheating nearly destroyed me, who abandoned his daughters, sending them into promiscuity and drugs. No, I choose to think that my heavenly Father had greater plans for me, but my choices and the choices of others got in the way.

That's just the way it is. No other explanation will do.

In the midst of a life, those storm clouds appear for whatever reason, and they do get our attention, don't they? Let's face it, we're a captive audience that way.

Desperate for answers, Ginger got none from her husband. He wanted out of the marriage and offered no explanation.

Her voice suddenly went hoarse. "I thought he belonged to the Lord. Now I'm not even sure of that."

I gulped. That's always hard to hear. "He'll have to answer to God for his choices. We all do." I thought it a good time to bring up the passage from Matthew 5:45, which says that God causes His sun to rise on the evil and the good, and sends rain on the righteous and the unrighteous.

We often get caught in a storm we can't harness. There is nothing to do but take cover in God's comfort until it's clear again. We still get sopping wet, but the downpour will not drown us.

I shared a favorite Scripture with Ginger. "Do not be afraid of sudden fear, nor of the onslaught of the wicked when it comes; for the LORD will be your confidence" (Prov. 3:25 NASB).

She seemed to respond slightly and filled me in on more of her story.

Ginger had always been a homemaker. She had raised their two sons, and while she wore the assistant hat and helped to run her husband's chiropractic supply office, she found identity and contentment as a wife and mother. Now, faced with all the practical matters of life, her seams were coming unraveled. Through his lawyer Ginger's husband insisted she enter into vocational training and get employed immediately.

He wanted to end the spousal support.

"All of a sudden, I'm a burden," she said with a long face. "After twenty-five years! How does he expect me to just pick up and start a career now? I'm so scared, Jan." Her voice cracked. "I can barely function through the day, let alone think of working."

Of course not.

Facing a crossroads like this, we are too exhausted to consider our "choices." In this state it's not easy to concentrate for very long. We're running on empty, unprepared to cope, and powerless to undo the damage to our dreams.

Have you ever echoed Ginger's words? "I hardly know what to expect from God now."

I have, and those familiar words brought a lump to my throat.

The first step in healing is to grasp exactly what loss does to us. Popping up from the table, I grabbed my tattered old Bible from the wicker basket near the sofa and returned to the kitchen table.

Flipping the worn pages, I read Joel's description of the locust plague and drought that consumed the land: "It has laid waste my vines and ruined my fig trees. It has stripped off their bark and thrown it away, leaving their branches white" (1:7).

"That's exactly how I feel," Ginger said, wide-eyed. "Stripped. In one fell swoop I lost my husband, my in-laws, my church. My sons are distant from me, too. It's as if my whole life was devoured."

She took to shopping out of town for groceries and avoiding her home church because "too many inquiring minds" wanted the lowdown on what happened to the model couple. "It's just too painful to tell all our friends he's left me," she said, biting her lip. "Now I'm just another statistic. I feel like such a failure. I'd rather die than be tossed away like an old shoe." She hoped to spare her parents the truth but finally admitted to her mother that her husband left.

"He probably wanted a younger woman," she told her daughter casually.

Any holes about my size to crawl into? Ginger wanted to know. For weeks she had roamed in a hypnotic daze around the house, just like a sleepwalker. "I didn't know how to wake up." Three or four times a day she walked past his closet to see if it was still empty but spent most of her time under the covers.

With a steady cramp in her stomach, her heart clumped in her throat, eating was impossible. "At least I'm getting thin now," she said. "Too bad he's not around to see it."

Ginger almost chuckled. A chuckle is always a good sign.

Hibernation is just a bit of beauty sleep.

The sleepwalking time conjured up memories for me. Days I can't even remember, going through the motions; I would awaken and attempt to eat, but nothing tasted good, and then I'd sleep while the kids were off to school. It's the logical response to a frontal attack. As the soul-attackers swarm and ransack, we have to latch the doors and windows of our heart and soul. It's as if God, in His mercy, numbs us from a reality that's too overwhelming to confront.

I'm sure you remember the story of Sleeping Beauty. After the princess was born, the entire kingdom brought gifts for the royal couple. An old grizzled fairy then spat a curse—that the princess should have her hand pierced with a spindle and die of the wound.

A young fairy stepped right up and announced, "I have no power to undo entirely what my elder has done, but rest assured your daughter will not die. She shall, indeed, pierce her hand with a spindle; but, instead of dying, she shall only fall into a profound sleep, after which a king's son shall come and awaken her."

She will fall into a deep sleep where she will have nothing to fear.

Let's call this a "soul siesta." A time to escape the heat, to hibernate from the pain. The trance-like time allows us to gather strength to continue the battle. It truly is a form of beauty sleep.

And don't forget what happens. A King's Son comes to awaken us, *to restore us to life.*

I told Ginger about Emily, whose life hit an iceberg when her husband died. "I spent two years in a state of deadness," Emily said. "But through the prompting of the Spirit of God and His love, the Lord wooed me back."

The next verse I read from Joel brought moistness to her eyes. "Mourn like a virgin in sackcloth grieving for the husband of her youth" (Joel 1:8).

Does it encourage you that Joel urged the people of Judah to weep for their loss, for the ruined vines and fig trees that were a staple in the Jewish diet?

Tears are cleansing to the soul.

When you finally wake up to the reality of what is happening, it's often hard to look at the remnants of a life that is about to change. For Ginger and Emily it was facing aloneness; for you it may be something very different. It still hurts like nothing you could have imagined. You need the freedom to mourn, to let the shredded emotions loose in a safe place.

I hope you will seek a refuge where your tears are warmly received. Ginger trusted me with her tears that morning. I merely supplied the tissue.

RAIDERS OF THE DARK

Humor me for a moment while I impart some of my research results.

Did you know there are eighty varieties of locusts? There are black ones, honey ones, and borers. They're members of the grasshopper family; drab, harmless, short-horned insects, living happy, solitary lives until their spaces get too crowded. Then watch out. It's a Jekyll and Hyde personality change. Excited and restless, the newly hatched hoppers cop an attitude, congregate, and hold a rally. Their eagerness causes a complete makeover, a color change to red and yellow with black markings.

Imagine what it was like to see hoards of them approaching? It had to be one of the most feared things in all the ancient world. Even today they are marauding Africa and Australia in record numbers and can move a hundred trillion strong. A typical swarm can be thirty miles long and five miles wide, threatening everything in its path.

Even laundry. Now this is insect trivia worth noting. These guys eat anything green that gets in their way, including clothes on the line.

Greedy little monsters, don't you agree? Attacking my crops is one thing, but my prized Liz Claiborne blouse that cost forty dollars on sale? Now that's something to avenge.

When God used locusts in the Bible, He did it to demonstrate His power. He unleashed them to humble Pharaoh into letting the Israelites go free from slavery. But beware: He sent them as warnings to all His people, so they could see and experience what He would do.

Imagine the stories these folks had to tell their children and grandchildren about what God had done for them! Here lies the point: Let the lesson be for all who come after us.

Old Pharaoh, what a stubborn gent! For the sake of one hardened heart, innocent people suffered all over Egypt. It's an odd thing about sin and rebellion. Others get mowed down in the wake of it like a runaway tractor.

It happened to Ginger, to me, maybe to you. And, of course, the green blouse on the clothesline.

As repulsive as they were in Bible times, disasters like this had one redeeming quality; they turned the people to God.

"I don't feel God with me right now," Ginger muttered. "He seems to have disappeared somewhere in the rubble."

All of a sudden this soft-spoken woman lashed out at the Lord. From tears to tirade. "Where is He? Has He deserted me? Why did He let this happen? I loved and served and prayed, and He let this happen. Why?"

Have you experienced these thoughts? Do you ever wonder where the God is who cares what happens to *your* bruised heart? It's OK. God isn't shocked to hear any of this or to know your faith is shaken. Not in the least little bit. Riding in the ambulance with her husband, Emily cried out in horror, "Oh, God, where are you in all this?"

"God never seemed more far away than at that moment. I felt so totally disconnected from Him. My deep anger toward Him for what I perceived to be a great betrayal brought my spiritual life to a screeching halt."

Look at the psalmists. They poured out their honest feelings. Isn't that a tender offer for us to do the same? To be honest about our feelings is not to be unspiritual. Jesus responded to His pain with loud cries and tears, and so can we.

Suffering is part of the Christian life. Affliction can be a treasure, it is often said, and the pain of life brings richness with God. But from experience I know that the newly hurting heart is just a tad slower to embrace this, to fully accept that pain is God's chisel for sculpting a life.

I pulled out a poem by Ruth Bell Graham stored conveniently in the flaps of my Bible cover for my times of temporary relapse. (I still get them even today.)

> I lay my "whys"
> before Your cross
> in worship kneeling,
> my mind beyond all hope,
> my heart beyond all feeling;
> and worshipping,
> realize that I
> in knowing You,
> don't need a "why?"[1]

That quieted her down a bit.

We talked about getting the answers in God's own time; eventually we see that trials come to teach us, and we begin to accept them as blessings.

But, meanwhile, how do you make the pain go away? Ginger wrestled with that question in my recliner rocker all afternoon.

There are no pat answers. Believe me, I searched high and low many times but came up empty. If they existed, I'd know what to do: I'll package them cleverly in refrigerator magnets and call the collection "Recipe for Restoration."

Hurting? Take Psalm 147:3 after breakfast ("He heals the brokenhearted and binds up their wounds") and jog down to the coffee shop for a double mocha.

I don't find much to watch on television these days, but I'm wild about the Home and Garden Channel that airs on cable. One of my pet programs is *Smart Solutions*. In a half hour I can discover clever ways to combat household problems: I've learned how to erase water stains on wood furniture, how to save plastic berry baskets to store my forever missing screwdrivers, and how to whip up a quick slipcover for the sofa the cat used for her nail file. Quick cover-ups, fast formulas, smart solutions. The show presents them nonstop between commercials.

But there are no smart solutions for this trek, I'm afraid.

Each of our inner shatterings is ours alone, and each loss is a unique mosaic of feelings and responses. Your path to restoration may take a different twist than mine. What we do share is the badge of our disappointment, the sign that we've known sorrow.

I urge you, don't fight it. Don't challenge God to spiritual arm-wrestling. Let the process come, and welcome it for as long as it takes.

Ginger wasn't certain she was ready to accept that. "I have to sleep on it," she said. "My head is spinning with all of this."

After she left, I spent time in prayer. *Lord, give her hope, even as she sleeps.*

Hope is the first line of defense against loss. Hope that eventually the swarm will be diffused and the attackers will go back to their solitary, nonaggressive life. Hope that, after some time has passed, the dawn will come again. It will peek up over the horizon in tiny glimpses of light. First, only as tiny as pin pricks, but each day they will grow wider until the bleak darkness isn't nearly as threatening anymore.

In a very old book on my shelf, *No Pat Answers*, Eugenia Price reminds us that hope doesn't come from God—it is *in* God.[2] If you feel distant from Him, the reason may be that you're waiting in a "hope" line with basket in hand, expecting a huge heavenly portion magically to drop in and lift your mood.

If only such a remedy existed. That's not how hope works.

Today's locusts are visiting us in new ways. Through marriage failures, sudden death of loved ones, financial failures, discouragement, guilt, and depression.

They are trying to spoil the spiritual harvest.

Know one thing: God is involved in your disappointment, your grief, and your struggle, and has a purpose for them, if you will permit Him to show you.

Here's the glitch.

There is no easy fix, no magic wand coming your way. But God isn't leaving you to fend for yourself. He doesn't plan on being an inactive accomplice in replanting your fields, sitting on His throne somewhere up there directing you while you toil through this mess.

Jesus said, "My Father is still working" (John 5:17). He's the original Master Gardener, up before daybreak, rolling up those sleeves, ready to dive in and break up the dirt clods. And this is a partnership, you and God hitched to the plow.

I love that image—us with God shoulder to shoulder.

Will you let Him take the lead no matter how long the plowing takes? It's about giving up control, the very thing you feel you're losing minute by minute.

Ginger still wrestled with this the next time we met at my house. She wondered—could there be a shortcut to the waiting, a balm for the ever-growing pain, something she could conjure up herself?

I shook my head but made no comment. Oh, how I wanted to give her some hard-earned advice! Some startling facts. Soon you may be tempted—you probably will—to sell your dreams for pennies on the dollar. Trust me, it may look like a solution, a way to remove you from your situation, but don't be deceived. God has plans to use this pain and loss, and He'll reward you far better than you can imagine, if you wait on Him.

But in her darkness she still couldn't see any light, and I had not earned permission to dole out the red alert, not yet. I was there to listen and share stories of others who had walked in her pain, who have moved from suffering to survival to service.

That's what she needed.

In his book *You Gotta Keep Dancin'*, Tim Hansel says that pain and suffering bring us to a fork in the road. It's not possible to remain unchanged; you either allow pain to corrode your spirit or allow God to transform you into the image of Christ.[3]

That's a tall order, wouldn't you say? But look at the alternative.

In Jesus Himself there is a clear explanation of life's tragedies. Later I knew that Ginger would grasp it all, but she needed to gain back some trust in God, to believe that she would sharecrop this wasteland with Him.

"But how long will this take, bottom line?" she inquired with a wince.

I raised my eyebrow and gave her a scant smile. Now that's a million-dollar question. Each person's timeline is different, depending on the circumstances, and the way you decide to wait.

True patience is accepting a difficult situation without giving God a deadline to remove it.

Gulp. I wish I had developed patience way back when. It took me five years to heal, but that's what happens when you insist on a major detour to avoid the pain, when you ignore the signposts that point to safety for the soul.

DETOUR THROUGH THE DESERT

What the locust swarm has left
the great locusts have eaten;
what the great locusts have left
the young locusts have eaten;
what the young locusts have left
other locusts have eaten.

—Joel 1:4

SOMETIMES I FANTASIZE about how the course of my life would have changed without the mishaps that blindsided me.

Enter Bob, my hero. He came sauntering into high school drama class, his flippant jokes a cover for the uncertainty of being the new boy in town. We practiced scenes from *Oklahoma* over and over until we became the parts. I had no doubts I would land the part of Ado Annie, the second lead in the musical, the charming scatterbrain who sang, "I'm just a girl who can't say no."

I didn't get the part, but I did get Bob.

After high school he joined the army, setting his sights on officer candidate school, and I went off to college. But the only book on my mind was The Book of Love: "Chapter one says I love him, I love him with all my heart. Chapter two says we're never, never, never, never, never, never gonna part."

Chapter three threw me for a loop.

While I immersed myself in college activities and dabbled in what dreams to pursue, Bob went off to a base in southern Germany. We wrote long and gooey love letters that year. I used all my pocket change to phone overseas, and we made plans for a white picket-fence future.

Then I came home for the summer, and a future bright with promise turned pitch black.

Since I was wholly committed to Bob, I found myself hanging out with my friend across the street and her new romantic interest, a sailor stationed at the naval base nearby. He seemed like a nice enough guy—witty, a good conversationalist. We all played endless games of cards, a good diversion for me.

One sultry summer evening the sailor rang my doorbell, asking to talk to me about his relationship with my friend. They'd quarreled. He needed advice. Could we go have a Coke?

How would I know he had no intention of discussing their romance? Call me naive, but I never guessed his real motives. Not until he drove me to a dark, deserted park and forced himself on me. It was all over so fast, I can't remember how it happened.

Today they call this "date rape."

I was only eighteen and now spoiled and ravaged. I blamed myself. How could I have allowed this to happen? Why didn't I scratch his eyes out when he first touched me? My young emotions and missing Bob's tender touch had fooled my common sense. Too stunned to think about the incident, I turned my thoughts toward going back to school a few weeks later. It could all be neatly forgotten, shoved into my past.

Until the rabbit died.

How could this be? Pregnant? Surely, this was not happening to me! It wasn't fair! I was a nice girl from a good family. I'd guarded my reputation so well.

I didn't know how to pray, but I asked (more like demanded) God to get me out of it, somehow. I couldn't tell my father, or he would have murdered the sailor.

The secret ate away at my insides like acid on battery cables.

Letters kept coming from Bob that I didn't answer. One night at 2 A.M. he phoned the dorm demanding an explanation for my silence. After he heard my story between the sobs, he said, "We're getting married right away."

"No, let me work this out myself," I said. Exactly how I didn't know, but marriage to Bob couldn't be the answer. The next weekend at home I confided in my friend. I warned her about the man she was opening her heart to, that he was not who he pretended to be.

In her own pain she refused to believe me and drew verbal swords. "You're lying! You must have seduced him," she said. I shrank back in horror. Could it get any worse? I'd lost my best friend, my virtue, and my white-picket fence future, all in one night. A victim of an unscrupulous, selfish jerk who denied it ever happened.

My mother could possibly handle the truth, but never my father, not in those days. What would the city mayor say to him? "Sorry, Newt, I can't support your bid for city council because, well, you understand, your daughter is in a bit of trouble."

So much for working it out myself. Bob's arguments finally wore me down, for his solutions made sense. I relented and agreed to marry him right away. "It'll be our baby," he said, melting my heart.

"No, we've got to have a fresh start." I insisted on giving the child up for adoption, certain I could never live in peace with *his* child in my arms.

So Bob hopped an Army transport plane and came back to California from Germany ten days later. Walking down the aisle in the Methodist Church of my childhood I had a disturbing tug at my heart. Was this any way to start out a marriage? With lies? A cover-up? A shotgun wedding? My mind raced with those thoughts while my feet took steps to the altar.

When I looked over at Bob in his sleek new suit, there stood my prince with his white charger waiting outside, ready to rescue his fair maiden from shame.

Maybe the tugs were only premarriage jitters. Who else would love me enough to do this? It must be the right decision.

Everyone thought we were off to Texas, but I went to Santa Barbara and stayed with a friend while Bob flew off to Germany. After the birth, I would hightail it overseas, and we could begin our fairy-tale marriage.

It was a perfect plan. Except of course, it wasn't God's plan.

I believed in God, and even prayed to Him regularly. I went to church on occasion, where my heart would stir at the words of the old hymns, and it felt refreshing. Yet there was never a friendship relationship with the living God through Jesus Christ, as I know it to be possible now.

Looking back, I can see how the Lord gently coaxed me, trying to get my attention up to the day of my wedding to divert me from disaster. In all the turmoil, it never dawned on me to consider Him or to ask God for guidance. Bob seemed to be the answer to my prayers.

Three months after my wedding, in a cottage by the Pacific Ocean, I went into premature labor and gave birth to a tiny stillborn girl who had suffocated hours before on the umbilical cord. When the nurse told me the baby had died, I shed no tears. *Thank you, God,* I ushered up, *for sparing me the pain of wondering about where this child would be.* The ordeal had ended. I could shut the door on the whole incident. I was truly blessed.

So I thought.

I came back to my hometown of San Leandro with a packet of lies to explain my sudden appearance. I applied for a passport, began packing my bags and brushed up on some German phrases. "Bavaria, here I come," I announced, bouncing through the house packing my bags. But they weren't going anywhere and neither was I. Bob received his orders for a tour in Vietnam.

Six months after Bob reported for heavy combat duty, his father committed suicide, and Bob was flown home on emergency leave for thirty days. In shock, he couldn't even cry. How could I let him go back to the war now? We had never started our life together, and future chances of him surviving in the jungles seemed very slim.

Believing in the merits of my plan, I asked my father to call on his contacts in the government and allow Bob to apply for a compassionate reassignment for the duration of his tour.

Bob didn't want to abandon his duty.

But surely, his duty lay with me now. I needed him. After pressure and whining from his new wife, he reluctantly agreed.

Spending the rest of his tour at the Oakland Army Base nearby, occupying his days dispatching the troops overseas, Bob ignored his misery. He repressed his anger toward his father, who had abandoned the family in Bob's youth and then ended his life without a word of goodbye to his son. He hid his disgust toward the Army for atrocities in Vietnam and his resentment toward me because I pressured him to stay home.

He was never my sweet, innocent Bob again.

Like many veterans he refused to discuss his battlefield experiences. Survivor guilt and shame wormed slowly through his heart and the secrets he buried.

Trouble spawned in him even then.

THE BUGS' BANQUET

One type of locust lives for years underground, emerges for one season, swarms, and then dies. They must be the kind that swept into my home. Hatched soon after our first kiss, the pests must have lain in waiting for the perfect time to surface in my life.

My dreams for a writing career went into limbo while I carved out a home for Bob and our two young daughters. I funneled all my emotional energy into balancing a difficult marriage. Restlessness plagued Bob, and he sought the thrill of other women. Each time a new affair surfaced, the wounds ripped me open. The scenario never changed. First came my discovery, then his guilt, followed by apologies, promises, and more promises. "Don't leave me. I don't know why I do it. I love you. It will never happen again."

Each time I felt my womanhood crumble and my trust shatter, but I felt bound to stand by him, forever. After all, he'd stood by me in my hard times, rescued me from shame. I owed it to him.

Didn't I?

Fortunately, I landed a part-time job at the local newspaper as a reporter. I turned to writing humor, and my weekly column, "Country Cluckin'," recounted funny yarns of our suburban family struggling with rural living. Readers actually laughed at my columns! I became a hit in our small community. Fan mail poured in. Could this be the launch of my writing rocket?

On a whim I wrote a novel, a young adult romance, and was referred to a New York agent who agreed to represent me. But when my mate said he had to leave me, that he'd finally found a woman he couldn't give up, and that I'd be better off without him anyway, I chucked the only copy of the manuscript in the trash.

If my dreams were going to ruin, it may as well be all of them.

A week after Bob left home, a station wagon rumbled up our dirt driveway in a screen of red dust. The chickens that foraged in the yard scurried for shelter, and the geese chased the rear tires, trying to jackhammer them with their beaks.

At least something was trying to protect the homestead.

A woman with a gentle smile kicked her booted foot at the geese and chuckled. She was undoubtedly no stranger to ranch life. When I answered the door, she said, "I'm Joyce," and offered me a warm casserole. "I read your column every week. Lately, I've had the feeling I should pray for you. Now I know why. I just heard what happened. I'm so sorry."

Flabbergasted, I groped for some words, but none came, just a little mew like the tiny cry of a baby kitten not sure which way to find warmth in the darkness.

The whole community must have known by then that the "country clucker's" husband left her for the 4-H leader, a supposed friend! I could imagine the whispers at the feed store. "Did you hear the latest?"

The other woman, the one who finally lured my husband from home, had helped me with our community 4-H club. She had taught my two girls competitive riding, and our daughters were friends. Just a few weeks before, she had told me she wanted to get to know me better.

Excuse me? My friendship antennas must have a fatal kink in it. "Come in," I squeaked to Joyce.

We chatted for a while about the geese, and then she said, "I have a Bible for you."

She flipped open the pages to some obscure passage from the book of Joel: "I will repay you for the years the locusts have eaten."

"It's a promise from God to His people," she said. "He'll rebuild your broken dreams if you trust in Him, Jan."

Locusts?

I have never liked bugs, but living in the country on twenty wild acres requires a certain tolerance for winged, hairy, crawling, buzzing, hopping creatures that turn up everywhere. They seem to have no good purpose other than entertaining some Rhode Island Red hens. It's hopeless to try and control them, especially when your daughter is a collector who never screws the Mason jar lids on tight enough.

But this image of an insect invasion drew a spark in me. An image of disaster and betrayal, swooping down on my life to dine and destroy. The dark sky, the buzzing drone, the fear and terror. As a writer, I couldn't have drawn a more vivid word picture. And God had some kind of answer for this?

My head tipped slightly with intrigue. "Can I read that?"

My eyes read further: "Return to Me with all your heart, And with fasting, weeping, and mourning; . . . Now return to the LORD your God, For He is gracious and compassionate" (Joel 2:12–13 NASB).

Fasting and weeping and mourning, that's what I'd been doing for weeks, crying out to a distant God I knew had to be up there somewhere, but I had no clue how to connect with him. As I read, my pulse quickened.

"Who knows? He may turn and have pity and leave behind a blessing" (Joel 2:14). There could be a blessing in this?

Joyce didn't beat around the bush. She told me, flat out, I needed the Lord to get through this. I needed Jesus in my life.

My heart pinched. She spoke the truth. I could never survive this wreckage alone. My own resources were dried up from trying to hold my marriage together for so long, from patching together my shattered self-confidence that I couldn't satisfy my husband, that somehow I had failed him, failed all of us.

"The threshing floors will be filled with grain; the vats will overflow with new wine and oil" (Joel 2:24).

How it would happen, I didn't know. When, I had no idea. But clearly God had sent this bold-and-gentle speaking woman to my door. Clearly He was pulling me toward Him. Though I couldn't trust the husband of my youth, God promised not to fail me. He'd replant my barren fields.

And so it began, my life of faith and locust self-education.

SIDESTEPPING IS A RISKY DANCE

Ginger sat motionless throughout the whole story.

"Can you relate at all?" I asked.

"Absolutely, especially when you talked about your anger and how you wanted to see Bob's body parts strewn all over the railroad tracks."

"I changed my mind about that. It's far too merciful an end. Chinese water torture is more appropriate."

It was the first time I'd seen her laugh since I met her. Humor helps.

"My neighbors tell me I should join a singles group," Ginger shot off as we stood in line for our toasted bagels a week later. "To help with the loneliness."

The hairs on my neck bristled. "Oh, Ginger. It's not a real good idea yet," I blurted out. "You are still married in God's eyes."

She frowned. "But I don't feel married anymore. Today I don't feel like I want him back at all."

In merely a week, she had mustered up a bit of spunk at least.

"No, of course you don't, and nobody expects you to. But the outcome of your marriage isn't the real issue here; it's how you respond to what God is going to do with your loss."

"Like what?"

"Restore you as a woman, His woman."

Her shoulders drooped.

"If your husband does come back," I continued, "if he's changed and wants to start your marriage over again, God will change your heart about him. It will be a brand-new relationship. And if his heart doesn't soften, God will set you free. You must wait and trust."

Wait and trust. How many times had I heard that myself?

Like steam from the coffee carafe, my mind drifted back to the week Bob left. I had fallen on my knees and asked the Lord into my life, not because I was thinking about eternity, where my soul would go after I die, but because I was at my wit's end trying to bat a zillion locusts off my property with one scraggly broom. God seemed to be the only sensible answer.

I had paced a path in the carpet a few nights before, struggling with the need to open a bottle of liquor in the cupboard to numb my pain. Images of my mother flashed through my head; my mother was often passed out drunk when I walked in the door from school as a child. She hid bottles all over the house. When life got too stressful, they became her comforter, and alcohol eventually killed her.

Could her daughter be headed the same way if she didn't get some help?

Then Joyce drove up the road. As she told me about another kind of Comforter, I knew I could get through the next hour, the next night, the next onslaught with Him.

A speck of green began to poke through the wasteland of my heart.

Wait and trust. Two small words with big consequences.

Bob noticed a difference in my life immediately. As I shared the Lord with him, he seemed eager to know more. A few weeks later, he admitted, "I want what you have. I need peace in my life."

Wow. Prayer works fast. Miracles happen. He moved back in, and we awkwardly tried to relate to each other. I watched him wrestle with his soul, be pulled toward God, even have a session with the pastor to ask all the questions about what a life with God requires. For a month he fought his inner voices, but the force of his desire to be with her was more than he could resist.

Call me old-fashioned, but I think husbands are like toothbrushes—they shouldn't be shared.

"Ask him to leave," my pastor said, "if he cannot honor your marriage. Living like this is too destructive." So I mustered up the courage to draw the line, to force him to choose. Trounced and beaten, I watched him pack his things. To my

horror, our twelve-year-old daughter Jennifer packed up, too.
"If you'd been nicer to Daddy, none of this would have happened," she snarled. "*She* loves me and wants to be my
mommy."

Trounced and beaten was a waltz compared to this.

As I watched my young daughter leave our home with her
father, I thought it must be a horror movie. This doesn't happen in real life. How did I mess up so badly?

There I stood, staring at more devastation than had come
with the first onslaught.

My daughter's rejection shattered my new faith. How could
it get any worse? Where was God in all of this? If the whole
community was praying for us, how could this happen? To top
it off, Jackie soon announced she was pregnant, a guarantee
that Bob would never come home to his family.

Where were these promises I had read about? This is a God
I should trust?

A 4-H friend, recently divorced, urged me to try going to a
dance to get me out of the house, to get my mind off my troubles. Why not? I could use some fun. Of course, my new
church friends were not consulted. I knew what they would
suggest. "Don't do it. Not now." I didn't want to hear it.

So I cut my hair, put lipstick on my face, and dusted off my
dancing shoes. Immediately I met a nice man I'll call "Mike"
who told me straightaway that he was a Christian. "Me, too,"
I said, and we had a great time talking about God, although I
pretended to know more than I did. Mike seemed to like me,
but as soon as he discovered my marital status, he backed off.

This is silly. What's a piece of paper, I thought? *My husband
is gone forever. I'm (gulp) free now.*

For the first time in months, I felt worthwhile as a woman.
A man smiled at me and danced with me, and I hummed an old
tune Carly Simon:

Haven't got time for the pain
I haven't got room for the pain
I haven't the need for the pain
Not since I've known you.

I hauled out my high school flirting diploma (self-presented) and set my hooks for this new acquaintance, convinced that God must have orchestrated the meeting.

Mike's wife had walked out on him, so we were comrades in that sense. Our growing "friendship" (that's what we dubbed it) cushioned me against more assaults—the custody battle and the revenge of a husband who now despised me because I attempted to defend myself in a custody suit.

Suddenly I became Bob's enemy.

Which drew me further into Mike's arms. We got very close as we talked and danced cheek to cheek, despite our pledge not to let things get out of hand.

With him, I felt safe and valued. I was on a reprieve from the battle—until we went too far, and I don't mean on a hike.

At thirty-five years old my intimacy had been stripped from me in my prime. My spirit and flesh were at their weakest, and I hadn't acquired the strength in the Lord to resist the yearning to be loved by a man.

Common sense went flying out the barn door.

It's funny how guilt and shame can be so camouflaged. Having fun and feeling desired masked the wrongness of the relationship. Though my girls despised his presence in our lives, I needed him. He suggested we get married.

Married? Picture me in a panic. I searched for love to touch up my bruises, not to tie any knots. It didn't feel right at all.

At the time I was attending a weekly women's study called 3-D: Diet, Discipline, and Discipleship. (Having fun had put a few extra pounds on me.) I decided to bring the issue of Mike's proposal before the group after our weigh-in.

Bless this group of women! Shocked as they must have been at my confession of immorality, not one of them condemned me. As a new believer, I'd never read verses like 1 Thessalonians 4:3, where Paul says it is God's will that we avoid sexual immorality and that we should learn to control our own body "with sanctification and honor, not with lustful desires."

And then there is verse 8: "Therefore, the person who rejects this does not reject man, but God, who also gives you His Holy Spirit."

Whoops. I certainly had never thought of it as passionate lust; it had to be love, right? Clearly, it was wrong in the eyes of God, whatever we called the expression of our feelings for each other. And by ignoring this mandate, I was thumbing my nose at God.

Truly, Lord? Do you mean that our bodies are like toothbrushes, too, not meant to be shared except within the sanctity of marriage? Should I marry him to make it right? Why did it feel so wrong?

These Bible study women wouldn't let me sit on the fence. They gently loved me into obedience, into yielding to God's nudge that I let this man go.

Somehow God seemed to be saying, "It's him or me right now, Jan. I want to restore you to wholeness. It will be delayed if you run into another marriage too soon. Hear this; the good is often the enemy of the best. I want to give you the best."

For weeks I battled with God and my emotions. Deep inside I knew one thing; on the outside I functioned just fine (after all, I was a great actress), but on the inside I was one messed-up woman.

Who am I now? I hardly knew anymore. Finally, girded up by my 3-D group, I broke it off with Mike, with one request— would he give me six months to sort things out? Stomach in my throat, I thought I would die without this man. "Why is this so difficult?" I blurted out during prayer-request time at the next meeting. "Because," the ladies answered gently, "two become one flesh, and when you separate, there is a harsh tearing."

Shredded again.

For two years I had sought to be loved to soothe my pain. For two years I had missed out on important healing time and togetherness with my daughters. (Jennifer had come back in pieces from her father's new home after six months, a very toughened and angry girl. Amy never complained but felt quietly neglected while I focused on the relationship with Mike.)

Mike decided against waiting and found someone else.

Betrayal, rejection, abandonment. Back in the emotional barn where all my previous losses were stored, I revisited the pain once again. And this time it was much more intense.

The swarm had sent out for reinforcements, and I had only one to blame. I had invited this plague myself.

One example is worth a thousand arguments.

Ginger tilted her head slightly and heaved a big sigh. "Wow. I had no idea." She pondered it for a moment and said, "I know what you tell me is true. You've been through so much, but look at you now. You have a good job in a senator's office. You're in ministry, always out doing things, having fun. Will I ever get there, be like you someday?"

Hopefully, she would choose to get there by a different route, avoiding the trap I fell into and the detour I took.

My task was to help her focus on God, not on me. What I'd been through should only help point her in the direction of the One who could manage the makeover.

"Well, if that's what you really want, I have to ask you to stick with me the whole way. Can you do that? Will you do it?"

And Lord, help me be up to the job.

So the rubber meets the road right here. Most of us *will* survive our loss, eventually, but to emerge as a *whole* person requires a conscious choice. First, you must embrace the pain, every last ounce of it, and let God transform it into the strength you need. The devil will tempt you, that's what he does when we're about to embark on the high road. You can find yourself in a battle where the enemy of God's restorative work will throw darts inflamed with lies such as these: *God can't do what you're asking. It's too hard to wait. You've messed up too much.*

What may look like security and safety, relief from the pain, can be a disguise for sin and self-destruction. Not just with a man, either. It can be anything that diverts you from the course God wants to take you on right now.

You have to trust God simply because He is who He is. You must understand that there are things you may *never* understand and still accept His already prepared journey, one small step at a time. Cling to the truth that Joseph tells his brothers who sold him into slavery. "'You meant evil against me, but God meant it for good'" (Gen. 50:20 NASB).

Even if it's hard to swallow right now.

"I want to learn to trust again," Ginger muttered, mascara streaking down her cheeks. "Trust that God does have a new purpose and new direction for me. It's just so hard right now."

I began to hum a favorite song of mine inspired from Philippians 1:6: "He who began a good work in you is faithful to complete it . . . faithful to complete it in you."

That day we made a pact and forged a friendship that would last a lifetime.

Ginger was anxious now to hear the stories of other women who experienced similar "air raids" in their life: Susan, whose husband's death sparked a series of disastrous choices; Linda, whose baby daughter was left disabled by an auto accident; Renée, who lost her teenage son; Natalie, whose abortion almost destroyed her; Liz, who spent years looking for love in all the wrong places—and many more.

God restored these women in ways they never dreamed, yet their pilgrimage to wholeness was no cakewalk. Restoration is a demanding venture. It takes all you've got.

It means submitting yourself to what I call a "whole life lift." You'll be scrubbed, plucked, buffed, pierced, and polished. And finally dunked in a mud bath to refine and purify.

It takes a bit of backbone to stick with this program, but the good news: it doesn't cost a thing, only your time and willpower.

Beware my friend, there is always the lure of running to another cure, a lover to soothe the pain, a new location to hide from the past, or pills to escape the future. Worse yet is Limbo-Land, a black hole where you settle into a pattern of anger, blame, and bitterness toward God, where you rewind and replay the hurts over and over.

You can't have rosy thoughts about the future
when your mind is full of the blues about the past.

I've asked myself where my life might have gone had my trouble not come. *What if I had never married in haste to escape my shame and fear? Would I have gone on to become a broadcast journalist? Would I have begun a writing career years ago? Would I have married a man who valued our marriage and his daughters? Would my children have suffered as much because of my senseless wrong turns?*

Who can know? But this I can tell you—because of the grace of God, I am not the woman of yesterday nor the woman I may have become if the circumstances were altered. But I am pleased with the Jan that God is molding me to be and with the finishing touches He is constantly adding to my life.

Because of this, my story is worth telling, for the difference it may make for someone else. It's not a story about losing a love but about embracing loss and finding new purpose.

Your story will be worth telling when the time comes, and believe me, you'll be asked to share it many times by women who need to hear the way you conquered your fears and doubts.

In the Old Testament Job is a good example of perseverance. He asks, "Where then does wisdom come from? Where does understanding dwell?" (Job 28:20). He then reveals that God alone knows where it is.

Here's my hunch: God has stashed a heap of it in the fallow ground of our ruined dreams.

Yes, we have to dig in the hardpan for a good while and break up the dirt clods with chafed but willing hands. Then grind out the old roots of regret.

Only then we will begin to find it.

Listen to what William Wordsworth said long ago: "Wisdom is often nearer when we stoop than when we soar."

CHAPTER FOUR

THIS FAIRY TALE IS A CLIFFHANGER

Surely the joy of mankind is withered away.
—Joel 1:12

UP AT GINGER'S MOUNTAIN HOME a few days later, I tossed out the question, "Do you remember the song 'When You Wish Upon a Star'?"

She offered me a raised eyebrow and a puzzled look. "Isn't that a Disney tune—from *Peter Pan* or something?"

"*Pinocchio.*" I was quite a Disney nut growing up.

"Oh, that's right. The cricket's song."

We chuckled in unison. We can't get away from those bugs, can we?

Her eyes flickered. We took a spin on a memory merry-go-round back to our childhood. What little girl doesn't relish fairy tales: graceful princesses, heroes on white horses, brutal beasts, and witches to battle "once upon a time"?

We crooned the words we could vaguely recall: "If your heart is in your dream, no request is too extreme . . ."

Is Jiminy Cricket's claim that no request is too extreme really true? Really?

Flashback to my childhood home. 140th Avenue, San Leandro, California. A safe, quiet suburb in the Bay Area. Cracker-box cottages all in a row. Houses mortgaged on the GI Bill by World War II veterans determined to make a "home sweet home" for dozens of baby boomer children that soon scooted and skated through the neighborhood. All girls, save one, and he says he wouldn't have missed growing up there for the world.

Summer nights found us romping on the bermuda grass of any front lawn, playing make-believe, building castles in the air with our unleashed imagination. One evening I saw a star shoot across the glittered, charcoal sky, and to my delight, nobody else spotted it.

Not that time, anyway. It was all mine to wish on. "Catch a falling star . . . never let it fade away." Another popular song that played at our house a lot in those days.

I never believed the moon to be made of green cheese, but I took it for gospel that wishing on a falling star was something amazing. Eventually I accepted the raw fact; the phenomenon is really a meteor. But when you're a wide-eyed and wishful thinker, it's a magical forecast of good luck—much better than coins in a fountain or finding a four-leaf clover.

Of course our dreams will come true. Our hearts are counting on it.

Ginger and I discussed how we treasured fairy tales as little girls. "I wonder where they came from?" I asked.

"I read somewhere that they came from salons of the French noblewomen."

So while these ladies had their wigs coiffed, they passed along the myth and folklore from their childhood? Yes, I could buy that. Cinderella, Sleeping Beauty, Rapunzel. Glamorous rags-to-riches stories.

But now it seems that some modern scholars claim such tales have underlying symbolism. Authors like the Brothers Grimm and Hans Christian Anderson were merely voicing their views on the politics of the day: "Shame on that oppressive moral code and down with the power struggles between classes."

Whoops. How did I miss that?

And what about L. Frank Baum? In crafting *The Wizard of Oz*, say the scholars, his purpose was not to reinforce the sweet thought that "there's no place like home," but to reveal a picture of a socialist alternative to American capitalism.

Huh?

I don't know about you, but I resent their taking away my harmless fantasy. I need to believe in Dorothy, the innocent dreamer who is swirled from Kansas into a Technicolor wonderland "somewhere over the rainbow." Every time I watch the movie I share her zeal to get to Oz, to convince the great Wizard to help her find the way home.

What could be more fun than to cozy up to a good fairy tale when you're a child? It's grand entertainment, the chance to let the imagination fly in a magic land of good and evil, storm clouds and sunshine, rainbows and romance. On some profound level the stories helped us cope with our world. They gave us the hope that we, too, could one day live happily ever after.

If only we believed.

Why is it that we never find unfulfilled dreams, shattered hopes, and discouragement in these stories? Why is it that only wicked witches melt into nothingness and eat the apple of their own destruction? The good girls always remain innocent; the fair maiden's yearning for the prince on the white horse always comes true. Do unforeseen storms ever drive these characters off course or tornadoes send them into the unknown for very long?

Not for more than a few hours or a few dozen pages. And that only makes the story more exciting.

Before we ever open the book, we know how it will end, with a happily ever after.

But one fine day on the way to womanhood the truth sifts through our fantasies. We realize they're all myths, little patches of fiction. But who cares? We still cherish those stories.

Castles with turrets and towers and secret passageways and broad moats to hold back the evil enemy.

DREAMS DO SCREAM

I had dozens of dreams growing up. I saw myself with a happy family, living in the country, surrounded by tall trees, a wonderful vegetable garden, horses to groom. I would write screenplays and novels at night in front of a grand stone fireplace.

Gone with the Wind remains to this day my favorite book and movie. Since I first saw it on the big screen at its re-release when I was a young teen, I knew that a Rhett Butler with mischief in his eye (but a heart of gold) would someday sweep me off my feet, and we would be together forever. We would have adorable curly-haired children and live the fairy-tale life.

My Rhett Butler did whisk me into his life, and I trusted him despite his roving eye. He would grow out of it someday, find himself, and settle down. My girls were most adorable, and there was plenty of time to write that screenplay.

Did you ever read horse books and dream of owning a dark, sleek one? I saw myself like young Liz Taylor in *National Velvet*, with undying faith in a winner against all odds. When our family moved to that plot of raw ground in Greenwood, wild with huge native oaks older than the California Gold Rush, dense with manzanita sprigs of dark wine red, we shared a dream—to carve out a homestead, scythe and chop, plow and spade, trench and irrigate until the land was tamed.

Just Ma and Pa and the girls. A little house in the big woods.

After fencing the first part of those twenty acres, we bought a horse and then added a pony. I passed my dream down to my daughters and watched them train their horses for gymkhana competition. I crossed my fingers and began to relax. Maybe the country life would be the tonic Bob needed to settle his soul.

This may work out after all.

Animals filled the pens, neat patches of green grass filled the landscape, and contentment filled Bob as he wore the hat of the gentlemen rancher.

Oh, how a land of milk and honey can turn bitter overnight! When he left us, suddenly my girls' sweet dreams dissolved like sugar cubes in scalding hot tea.

How could he do this?

Dreams never die easily. Though they may be ruined, your precious dreams won't melt away like a popsicle in August. Dreams are the fibers of who we are, the textures woven in and through us. We've spent much of our waking hours weaving these dreams, giving them form and definition.

When you're in a crisis, you'll be given all kinds of advice. Many will be glad to interpret for you what's going on, and you'll hear many voices telling you what to do. "Give it up. Move on to something else." "A change of scenery will do you good." "Clean out the closet, get rid of the memories."

It's crucial to listen closely to God, not to people right now. "For my thoughts are not your thoughts, neither are your ways my ways, declares the LORD" (Isa. 55:8).

What may seem like common sense might not be at all.

We usually don't give up the dream without a fight. To hang on is as natural as a Banty hen protecting her new chicks. It's tough to let go until we're certain there will be something else; another dream will take the place of the one destroyed by the gluttony of grief, betrayal, and regret.

It's OK. You don't have to let go yet.

For two years I clung to that plot of red clay dirt and rolling hills, to that parcel filled with craggy digger-pine trees, to that boxy manufactured home in the Sierra foothills. I struggled to make the payments (Bob had a convenient way of avoiding support), sold off the beloved animals one by one, and watched the lush garden go to weed. The hard winter rains flushed the gravel off the dirt road, turning it into a furrowed motocross course.

Ruined dreams scattered the landscape.

> *Flowers grow out of dark moments.*
> —Anita Corita Kent

I needed a job at this point, as my hope and money were running pretty low. I couldn't support us with my part-time work at the newspaper.

Dusting off my rusty high school typing skills, I scoured the want ads. When I found one for a "secretary with writing skills," I eagerly sent off my résumé and shrieked with joy when a state senator's office called to set up an interview.

As I sat across from the chief aide, my ears perked up at the job description—writing and dealing with constituent problems. Finally, something seemed to go right. For the first time, I saw a glimmer of hope.

As I left the office after an hour, a huge sigh of pleasure escaped me. It had gone better than expected. The elevator gracefully opened as if to congratulate me. This job was mine. Tailor-made for me, I knew it. If I had to work, I prayed it would be a match for my skills and interests.

When the official-looking letter came a week later, I ripped it open. "While the decision was a difficult one . . ." The letter told me I made a strong showing, and if it was any consolation, I was the second choice.

Second choice? That sounded all too familiar.

That night I wrestled with God. *Must I die to more dreams, Lord?* I read through Psalm 130: "I wait for the LORD, my soul waits and in his word I put my hope" (Ps. 130:5). The next day another job offer came, and though it met my financial needs, I knew I'd be miserable working there, so I turned it down.

"Are you sure that's wise?" my father asked.

"Sure," I replied, faking my confidence.

Two weeks later I had a message to call the senator's office. I clenched my teeth as I anxiously dialed the phone. I vaguely heard something about an "authorization paperwork jam" at the state level. The number one choice couldn't wait. Was there a chance I might still be available?

I may have been the second choice, but God had the last word.

The story may be a slight diversion, but it relays what the psalmist tells us about the attitude we're to have in times of painful waiting; when times are dark, we're being refined. Hang in there with certainty that He is full of surprises, that He'll meet your needs, and that you'll be planted where He chooses at the right time or place.

There is no need to panic and grab at something too soon.

Every day, going to work, I had to traverse the American River canyon that snakes over a six-mile two-lane highway through the foothills. Though I loved the job, every night on the hour-plus drive home, my tears stained my dress. How everything had changed! I had neither the time nor the interest to putter around the property, especially after a long commute.

Against the advice from my parents, I refused to make moving plans. I ignored pressure from Bob's lawyer that I sell the place and "divvy everything up."

He made the process sound more like a couple of gold miners abandoning their claim than a once-sacred marriage vow.

No way. I wouldn't budge, even though staying on the ranch kept me connected to a constant reminder of my pain and loss.

Of course, it was only a matter of time before the homestead would have to be sold. There was little energy or money left for maintaining the ranch. One morning, while the scrub jays jeered at the few scrawny chickens left in the pen, I found myself outside clutching a clump of red dirt, sobbing dramatically, "As God is my witness, I will never be hungry again."

A jovial Irish voice whispered in my memory, *Land, Katie Scarlett O'Hara. Land is the only thing that lasts.*

My head shook. *Hey, girl, you've watched* Gone with the Wind *too many times. It's make-believe, honey, and you're too old for that. So what if Scarlett ate radishes and killed an invading Yankee to hang on to her beloved home? You are not Scarlett. She is fiction; you are real. Besides, she married two wrong men to keep Tara, and she lost the right one due to her own stubborn shortsightedness.*

Well argued—I'm no Scarlett. I certainly didn't share her assurance that "tomorrow is another day." And I didn't leave my readers wondering how I would ever manage to get my man back and live happily ever after. My man was history, married to a woman about to have his third child. He had wasted years of my life while I stood by him through nightmares of Vietnam, senseless affairs, and dozens of business ventures he had to try.

Yes, he trampled my dreams, crushed them as if with massive bare feet on rich wine grapes. I had left Bob once when the girls were small, after his fourth affair, when the "woman" sent me a picture of the two lovers together. But my husband begged me to come back, promising it would never happen again. If our marriage had died at that time, wouldn't it have been so much easier on all of us? Why hadn't I listened to my parents and taken their offer to help me escape?

I rocked on the porch of regret.

What does that ever do? Nothing, except wear a deep groove in the floor. Back and forth, rocking over the same old territory but never getting anywhere.

Why is it so hard to let go of what might have been?

INVASION OF THE BRAMBLE SNATCHERS

When we were down to the last bale of hay, we had to find new homes for our horses. The girls were crushed but agreed we had no other choice. Almost immediately, yellow star thistle invaded the hillside pasture where the mares had once happily grazed. Star thistle is a superstar weed, a yellow prickly monster that grows in country fields. It is extremely toxic, except to the bees—they can turn it into the most fantastic honey.

This weed thrives on neglect, one of the few things that does. Soon, a golden sea of spiny flowers seized the ground around our home. It appeared like a billboard posting a notice, "Entering a Wasteland."

Mine.

Coping with my own prickly pain, I never went into that pasture again after our horses were gone. I avoided the garden too, the place where I'd been happy to dig and trowel, enriching the red dirt. Soon the gate hung off its hinges, and rust crept over the tools hiding in the weeds. Where nothing stirred—no prancing goats or foraging chickens or children's playful feet—the thistles took control.

The dream of country life had finally died.

The prophet Isaiah has comforting words for those who are dying to dreams: "The mountains and hills will burst into song before you, and all the trees of the field will clap their hands. Instead of the thornbush will grow the pine tree, and instead of the briers the myrtle will grow" (Isa. 55:12–13).

When our dreams slip out of reach, their disappearance tests what we believe. Trusting God means believing that His purpose is greater than our loss. It's knowing that He will use it as a tool to change and grow us. It means picking our way through the thistles into more confidence in God than we had before things got ruined.

Maybe there's another lesson here. When life gives you thistles, make honey.

Keep in mind that readiness to let go is often tardy. It lumbers along behind, waiting for the cue to take the lead so it can say, "Now follow me. I have new dreams for you."

There is a new place to go, somewhere over the rainbow.

A rainbow is more than an arch of colors in the sky; it serves as a promise that no matter what happens, God's mercy and grace will finally triumph. God said to Noah, "Whenever I bring clouds over the earth and the rainbow appears in the clouds, I will remember my covenant between me and you" (Gen. 9:13).

David tells us that "the LORD is faithful to all his promises and loving toward all he has made" (Ps. 145:17). God desires to create a rainbow highway for you right in the midst of the barren fields of your ruined dreams.

Your own yellow brick road. When you see it clearly, it's time to let go.

> *The way I see it, if you want the rainbow,*
> *you gotta put up with the rain.*
> —Dolly Parton

When we first bought the half-Arabian filly after moving to Greenwood, we decided to try and break her for saddle, giving the girls a chance to win her confidence. Every day nine-year-old Jenny would skip down to the pasture after school and slip a blanket on and off Sher's back until the horse trusted her touch. Next she had to allow the bit into her mouth, and finally she had to get used to the feel of a saddle. Watching the thousand-pound horse struggle, pull, and resist with Jenny gave this mother fits. What were we thinking? This was a strong, willful, dangerous animal!

But Jenny wouldn't give up. She stroked and coaxed Sher with gentle assurance. Each day the horse trusted a little bit more, yielded a little bit more, until she finally gave over her destiny to my daughter. Sher had come to understand that we would never hurt her and that she could trust us. We could almost see the moment when it all clicked and when she figured out that her new life might be an adventure. Saddled, she would be leaving the corral and exploring many new and wonderful places.

Yielding takes time.

Ginger began to understand this and how she would be changed by her loss. But like a little girl with a ragged teddy bear or a favorite blanket, she still needed to clutch to her dreams. She felt scared, anxious, frustrated, angry, and worthless all at the same time. Though her mate had snuffed out their future with his decision to leave, she couldn't move on yet. She had worked hard to get him where he was in his business, and now the kids were grown and on their own.

"This was to be our time," she said. "We made plans for the future. What will happen now? I don't deserve this."

God understands that you may have to let go of your dreams gradually, yielding them bit by bit, and that you may struggle against the change. The people of Judah certainly did when the locusts came and the trees of the field dried up. As Joel reminds us, "Surely the joy of mankind is withered away."

You are facing unfamiliar territory, and it's frightening to let go of a life you've counted on to risk the unpredictable, the completely unknown.

God only asks you to begin to trust Him in a new way with your new life. Like my daughter with her horse, God will gently love you into surrendering control, into releasing your dreams.

Each time I read *Gone with the Wind,* I shake my finger at Scarlett in the last chapter. Melanie has just died and with it also comes the death of Scarlett's dream of marrying Ashley. In the drawing room of the Wilkes's home, it finally dawns on her that she has loved something she made up, a dream born in childhood, a safe and comfortable haven. What a fool! It's Rhett she really wants, but remember how he responds: "My dear, I don't give a ———."

After our heroine wipes her tears (and bucks up like classic Scarlett), she vows to think about it tomorrow; she'll concoct a way to get him back. Don't you just want to shake the stubborn resolve from this Southern belle? Scarlett just doesn't understand that there comes a time to stop fighting for one's own way. Doesn't she see? The weaker and less sufficient we are, the more powerful God becomes.

I want to write my own sequel. Scarlett yields her life to the Lord when she retreats to Tara, and her new perspective and softened heart draws her man home.

I confess, I'm still a hopeless romantic.

CHAPTER FIVE

BLOOM AGAIN

The seeds are shriveled beneath the clods.
                                    —Joel 1:17

IT WAS SUPPOSED TO BE the Indian summer of Ginger's life, a time to enjoy the fruits of her marital harvest. Instead, the horizon remained dark. No skyline in view, no peephole through the black clouds, visibility not much above zero at this point.

The first thing I asked Ginger to do was write a hundred times on the blackboard of her heart these words: *It only lasts for a season.* We can all survive one season. (Come on—yes you can. We're here with you all the way.)

As self-proclaimed professor emeritus of the Bug Blight, I earned my degree the hard way. I know of what I speak.

It's not that I have a fascination with insects, but after I met these nasty ones eighteen years ago, I took some counsel from Dad, a World War II veteran of D-Day: Know your enemy. If the Allies hadn't studied Hitler's tactics, identifying the menacing forces that drove him and his military management style, it would have taken much more time, manpower, and supplies to defeat him.

Kay Arthur, author and founder of Precepts Ministries, agrees: "Throughout the New Testament God reminds us that we are in a conflict—not with flesh and blood but with principalities and powers and spiritual wickedness in high places.

Therefore, it's essential that you understand the tactics of the enemy so you won't be caught off guard."[1]

We need to be taught war, she reminds us.

Especially when we've grown up with the fairy tales, I want to add.

It's good to know that God is on our side, but we need to do more than crouch down and hide in the trenches, praying for a rescue or a cease-fire.

By reading God's Word, we can see that He has the battle plan for us completely laid out; I call it our "Scorched Earth Policy." Subtitle: "Holy Defensive Warfare."

When we first meet Joel the prophet in chapter one, he is addressing the citizens of Judah, and he is in a persuasive mood. "Hear this," he begins, speaking to them about the current problem and describing in cruel detail the impact of the locust plague. A dire situation, for these folks now have no grain to eat, nothing to sell, and nothing left to plant.

Depending on what Bible translation you read, Joel describes the insects descending on Judah as gnawing, swarming, creeping, stripping locusts, or as cutter, hopper, multiplier locusts. Then there are the swarmer, shearer, lapper, devourer locusts, all stages in the insect's life cycle.

Joel uses military terms as he writes, talking about the approach of the enemy: "A nation has invaded my land, powerful and without number; it has the teeth of a lion, the fangs of a lioness" (Joel 1:6).

The jaws of these psychotic insects are toothed like a saw. How else can they gnaw the bark off twigs after the foliage is gone? This doesn't sound like the harmless green katydids my youngest daughter used to capture and keep in a canning jar with nail holes in the lid.

Not harmless at all. They've demolished everything in Judah in 800 B.C. The fig tree symbolizes the nation of God's people and their spiritual privilege, yet it was all stripped to nothing.

Joel calls the nation to fasting and prayer, telling the people to "mourn like a virgin in sackcloth grieving for the husband of her youth" (Joel 1:8). He implores them to mourn as if they were experiencing the pain of unfulfilled love. Most of us can relate to that in some way.

Natalie certainly does, and I shared her story with Ginger. Natalie arrived at the legislative office to interview with me for my former position. (I'd been promoted to office manager!) Her nerves in a flutter, the urgent yearning in her eyes revealed how badly she wanted this job. I had no trouble casting my vote for her; she had all the necessary qualifications and a slight edge, our instant bonding. Soul sisters surviving the locusts.

Over lunches at the nearby pizzeria, we traded battle stories. In Natalie I found an authentic person, a woman who truly loved the Lord, willing to reveal her pain and anger. I'd been trying to keep mine under wraps at work, forcing plastic smiles even when I felt at odds with the world, giving my direct supervisor, our field coordinator, carefully rehearsed nuggets of faith when he asked me questions. (*I have to show him that with God I'm making it just fine*, I'd tell myself.)

Truthfully, the ground rattled under my feet. Single for three years by this time, I resented working full-time when my daughters were in crises, as they made dangerous attempts to process their own losses: getting suspended from school, dabbling in drugs, running away overnight with boyfriends, even experiencing a stint at juvenile hall.

When I met Natalie, I had just come out of my rebound relationship. Being obedient to God in giving this man up would make everything better and bring me some peace, wouldn't it? A little reward?

I deluded myself into thinking that by doing the right thing God would reward me on the spot. In my period of painful waiting, doubts filtered in. Would there ever be a healthy love in my future? Would I ever have a future? Would I be doomed to this limbo existence forever?

And then in waltzes Natalie with her khaki brown hair and marble-smooth skin peppered with girlish freckles. We could hardly wait until the office closed for lunch so we could jet over to the pizza place to shore each other up over bread sticks while waiting for the special of the day. (I could feel myself adding some flesh, but what did it matter? I was shedding some emotional fat with each bite I chewed.)

We exchanged stories of our ruined dreams. As a child Natalie had longed to be a veterinarian, to have her very own horse, to become a mom with at least five kids, and maybe to be a little rich. None had ever come true.

"I also wanted to be petite," she added, slapping her leg, "but no way with my fat thighs."

Those pizza lunches helped me to laugh at myself again.

Like millions of women, especially the baby boomers, she honestly believed that every childhood birthday and Christmas would bring the desire of her heart, her own horse. But it never came. "My dreams never materialize," she admitted to me. "I can lean far too much on the pessimistic side, probably stemming from the abandonment of my father when I was three. I feel as if good things happen to everyone else but never to me."

How well I understood the tendency for that self-prediction.

Divorce wasn't the greatest disaster for Natalie. The crushing knockout blow was infertility. Every month, twelve months a year for eight years, she endured shattering disappointment. "It undermined my sense of being part of the human race," she told me. "Like an acid, it ate away at my sense of being a complete woman—trying, hoping, praying, and believing, and not being able to accomplish deliberately what millions of women do casually." She jutted out her bottom lip slightly. "Even accidentally."

She might have been speaking about me.

As the thought dashed in, I swept it away. I hadn't told a soul about the incident before I was married, and I vowed to leave it buried in my past. But I was very vocal about my present situation, grumbling at the burdens of single parenthood and two confused, rebellious daughters. And yet my new friend ached over an empty womb, something I'd never known. What she tearfully said next made me push aside the rest of my Hawaiian pan pizza.

"I got pregnant before we got married, and my husband insisted I have an abortion."

I reached out and touched the sleeve of her silk blouse, and again I had no words. "I did get pregnant, finally," she said, "but the baby, Steven, died after eleven days. The doctors said there would never be another. The abortion had made it impossible. My husband left me a short time after, and he found someone who could give him a family," she choked.

Barren fields, barren body. She wondered how she could survive in the same town as her husband, an active attorney. Her face sobered. "I've thought seriously about a hit man."

My eyes rolled. Hadn't that thought crossed my mind a few times?

When I began writing this book, I contacted my dear friend and asked her to draw on the thoughts and feelings of that time.

"The torment of my infertility did such destruction on my heart. That was the gnawing locust swarm. They came, they stayed, they conquered," she said. She felt no prayers answered, no relief from God, no hope. She wished someone could assure her, "There dear, it's all right. God will fill the void. He'll provide the family you need to fill the picture of a real life that you have in your mind.'"

But God didn't fill that void. He did not provide the family Natalie so desperately wanted. "It's like an amputation," she said. "You learn to live without the limb, and you can get by OK, but it's never the same as when the limb was there."

One thing I respect about Natalie is her directness. "I don't like the attitude that some Christians take that 'Praise the Lord anyway' is the answer to loss. I believe we must first acknowledge the loss, then assess it, then discover God's plan in it. Praising God before understanding is, to me, foolish and dishonest."

She remembers well the day when she stopped battling, took a deep breath, and conceded defeat to infertility. There would be no family, no baby to hold, no scraped knees, no grandbabies. "I was prepared at thirty-five to redirect my life and try to figure out what I wanted to be when I grew up, because what I really wanted to be was somebody's momma."

It felt good to give up, shift her focus, cut her losses. "I was working in the pro-life movement at the time," Natalie recalled, "and I had a husband who needed me, and I would just move on. My life would not include children. An awfully hard mountain to climb, but I would climb it." Within a week or two of that revelation, her husband left and moved in with his secretary.

Then the storm began in earnest.

"After he left," she went on to say, "I tried everything I could to get him back, all the time knowing in my gut that he wasn't coming home. The loneliness was everywhere, the sadness all-consuming. It was unbearable to sit alone, knowing that my husband was with someone else."

When she read her Bible, she found herself in the Psalms. "Both the sorrow and hope that King David recorded there became my own close acquaintances, so it seemed less lonely somehow.

> *Though you have made me see troubles, many and bitter,*
> *you will restore my life again.*
> —Psalm 90:15

"I was panic-stricken. I bargained with God. I lost weight (what a way to do it!). Alas, after a couple of months, I was irresistibly drawn to other men. I was devastated, jilted, thrown over, abandoned, tossed aside, unwanted, and undesirable. Used goods. And being with a man who found me attractive was a strong temptation for me."

When she applied for a new job with the American Life Lobby in Sacramento, Natalie knew she would have to leave the old life behind to work for such an organization.

So she tried.

With the new job came surprised notoriety, being on television and radio with notables such as Dr. James Dobson of Focus on the Family. Working with important political people was, she admits, a baby step toward a sense of self-worth.

"God pointed me toward other people, toward an important cause near to my heart," she added. "I couldn't have babies, but I wanted to be a part of trying to save precious unborn lives."

A faithful friend is an image of God.

Friends are life preservers tossed to us on stormy seas. Natalie's new boss, John, became a trusted friend. He insisted she either begin regular church attendance or find another job. "The pro-life battle is a spiritual one," he told her, "and to be effective we need the support of a church family."

"Bless him for that!" she said emphatically.

Still there were times when the grief and loneliness were as new as the first day, and she still felt as though the darkness would never lift. "And there were days when I could almost feel myself growing strong. My emotional state was like the Incredible Hulk—remember him? When provoked, he started growing those huge muscles, and the seams of his shirt popped right out. He had this enormous strength he didn't realize."

Some days she would get up and think, "Today I don't hurt so bad. I feel strong, like I can make it, after all."

Most of the big bumps on Natalie's road to healing consisted of some trip-ups with men, she confessed. "It was a pattern I had before I was married, and it resumed during my new state of singleness. Most fortunate for me, God's mercy and grace are unfathomable and amazingly generous."

She read her Bible faithfully, but "I still sinned regularly," she interjected. "My spiritual growth mirrored my emotional growth, but I was gradually becoming a strong Christian and desiring more to please God than myself."

By the time we hooked up, Natalie had been through the worst of her storm. She had learned to forgive her former husband. "I realized that he was no more wicked than me, really. He just made some selfish, hurtful choices. Understanding that was a healing." Plus, she was beginning to accept that God had a purpose for everything she endured. "I started yearning for God's voice much more than a man's arms."

The girl was way ahead of me.

One day at lunch, she inquired, "Have you read Isaiah 54?" I wobbled my head no. I wasn't too acquainted with the Bible yet. So we had our first study over teriyaki chicken bowls. (We had tired of pizza by then and needed a culinary change.)

We read verses 5 and 6 together: "'For your Maker is your husband—the Lord Almighty is his name—the Holy One of Israel is your Redeemer; he is called the God of all the earth. The LORD will call you back as if you were a wife deserted and distressed in spirit—a wife who married young, only to be rejected,' says your God."

She explained to me that Judah in exile is viewed as a wife separated from her husband, God Almighty, but is eventually restored.

"'Your Maker is your husband. The LORD will call you back.'" My heart stirred at those words. *God as my husband?*

"I dwell on this truth every single day," Natalie said. "God will never abandon me, never betray me. He is my mate now."

She had come to that fork in the road, where she must either trust God blindly that He would give her the answers in His own good time or abandon all faith in Him.

"So after my private God-bashing, I claimed the promise that all things work together for good to them that love God.

I asked Him to work a miracle of bringing good out of the pillage that was left of my life."

This became our daily prayer for each other: "Lord, bring good from the pillage." We also found another promise from God in Isaiah 61:3, that He will bestow on us a crown of beauty instead of ashes.

Natalie's life was my first proof of it.

In this friendship God had thrown two opposites together—a solace-seeking introvert and a social butterfly always itching to find the party or create one.

"Won't you come to this singles' group with me?" I urged. "There's a big church here in town. They put on concerts on Friday nights with volleyball and fellowship after. A safe place to get out. Sound like fun?"

She always begged off, preferring quiet gatherings where she would bring out her guitar and strum praise songs to soothe our souls. God knew I needed Natalie to help me stay focused on growing and healing. Jumping into the singles' pool too soon would be a mistake. I needed to master some of the necessary lifesaving strokes, or I might drown again in my own foolish desires.

Natalie often invited me over for dinner after work, to show off her lush, thriving garden, where she invested most of her time creating an oasis of colors and textures that would make Martha Stewart drool. She had a blue-ribbon touch with flowers—sunset-colored cosmos, golden marigolds, wine red Dahlias, all hemmed by yellow purple-hearted pansies. Her garden smelled like a banquet hall full of prom queens with giant corsages.

The only plants thriving at my place were star thistle and poison oak.

"Flowers each have their own personality, don't they?" She clicked the pruning shears twice in her gloved hand as I nodded. She pointed out how the daisies are always so charming and the oriental poppies so dramatic, and how the petunias sprawl all over the place with no rhyme or reason.

I pursed my lips. Is this what happens when we're alone just a wee bit too long?

Pots bursting with color invited me into the patio, flowers with names I could never pronounce.

Snipping blooms from a yellow flower I couldn't recognize, she then said something I've remembered all these years. "You know, we can never be like these lilies unless we spend time as bulbs in the dark, totally ignored."

I plopped down in a weathered wicker chair and pondered the deep truth of that.

"Oswald Chambers said it first," she told me, cutting a bouquet for the table. "I'm passing it on to you for free."

Can new crops really sprout from desolate ground? In the dry fields full of withered seeds, we wonder if God is really good, if anything new and fresh will ever come out of the deep abyss of our loss.

It's in those dark, dry, lonely places that we thirst for His voice.

Natalie had made the Lord her husband, even when she couldn't trust or embrace Him fully, even when the relationship was awkward and distant because of her own inner battles. Even when He didn't seem near or caring. Somehow, some way, she would be restored.

Think of yourself just as a seed patiently wintering in the earth; waiting to come up a flower in the Gardener's good time.
—C. S. Lewis

Because Natalie was gaining a new sense of purpose through her legislative work in our office, she hardly noticed the handsome man visit her small church (in which she happened to be the only single woman) one Sunday morning.

Well, maybe she did notice him a little. She burst into work the next day, her eyes popping out of her head like Big Bird's.

Barely able to contain herself, she exclaimed, "This guy has such a gorgeous smile, and he seems so—normal!"

What a coincidence that this was the same church she began attending at the urging of her boss. Little did she know what lay in store as she committed to regular attendance there, but God did.

But let's not jump too far ahead.

"I lived their romance vicariously," I then told Ginger. "Every phone call, every lunch date, every time she braced herself at Jerry's mere mention of changing careers, or dreaming of starting a business in a small town somewhere. She was certain that their romance was only a flirtation for him."

A year into the relationship, Jerry accepted a job in the Bay area. He told her he couldn't commit to anything yet.

Naturally Natalie took a dive into Castaway Lake, where ruined dreams are often dumped. Trying to encourage her, I said, "Natalie, I know he cares for you, but this is a serious man, and he was a brand-new Christian when you met him. I think he wants to do the right thing by you and the Lord. He needs to sort this out before he makes a serious commitment. Nobody wants another divorce."

She gave me that "how do you know any of this" look, but I pressed on. Finally, she bucked up and got busy with God's work again.

"And? What happened?" Ginger couldn't wait to find out.

"Well, after nine months of complete silence, Jerry appeared at her door, telling her he'd resolved his past hurts and fears and had decided on what he wanted. It was incredibly romantic. They got married two weeks later at the end of a church service and moved two hours north of here. They settled in a quaint old farmhouse on twelve acres."

Ginger's eyes sparkled. "And I'll bet she finally got her horse."

"A horse? She's got three!"

And there's more. Natalie had gotten her teaching creden-
tial because, as she puts it, "I couldn't think of anything else to
do with an English degree except open a poem repair shop."
(Don't you love the wit in that woman?) It appeared that
Jerry's teenage son needed some serious coaching if he would
ever graduate from high school. With Natalie's help he got his
diploma. The word got around, and Natalie consented to help
a church mom "here or there" with home school and some
tutoring "now and then."

A decade later she is still "helping." This year she's holding
classes for twelve children from fourth through eleventh grade,
earning a small salary for her efforts. "I know this is the ministry God has intended for me, using my unique and God-given
skills and talents. I love these kids so much it surprises me, and
I know I'm assisting God-fearing parents in their efforts to
raise up children in the way they should go.

"Remembering back on those times, I simply can't identify
with that insecure woman any more," Natalie recently told me.
"I can say with absolute certainty that Jerry had the opportunity,
and hasn't squandered it, of teaching me what unconditional
acceptance from a man is all about. God has given me peace and
security and confidence with my life and my husband."

Could Natalie have scripted this beautiful ending? Could
she have planned this for herself?

And you'll love this one: The church where she first met
Jerry is the sister church to her current congregation, whose
children she's been teaching for ten years. She says, "I have
found blessings unnumbered."

How amazing and how unpredictable are His ways!

Being witness to Natalie and Jerry's love story tested me
more. As the skies cleared for her and the gentle rains began to
fall on the parched soil of her heart, my eyes were barely adjust-
ing to the dark. My seeds were still shriveled beneath the sod.

Every now and then I sensed some activity with the change
in my spirit, the settling of my mind, the acceptance that a new

life with less fear would emerge. But I still slogged in the muck; I was still fighting my battles—in court over the property and at home with my daughters as they looked for love in all the wrong places and confronted moral hazards with no caution. At sixteen Jennifer moved out, determined to make her own way outside my control. With the loss of her sister, Amy floundered even more.

The message of darkness is to teach us to lean on God.

Keep me centered in the dark, I prayed. During the storms, keep me in the eye of the tornado, give me calm assurance that you'll place me on stable ground someday.

Meanwhile I held firm to the promise that God wouldn't let the storm defeat me.

"We are pressured in every way but not crushed; we are perplexed but not in despair; we are persecuted but not abandoned; we are struck down but not destroyed" (2 Cor. 4:8–9).

Natalie had endured, and I watched her head out over the rainbow with a song in her heart, a mighty good man, and new dreams.

Designed by God.

I love telling her story. "I needed her at that exact time to help me understand how locusts ravage, and to plan a campaign strategy against them," I remarked to Ginger.

In Lamentations 3:2 Jeremiah says, "He has driven me away and made me walk in darkness rather than light." For what purpose? Because God knows that we grow the most in the dark.

When you're there, do what Oswald Chambers suggests: Listen and God will give you a very precious message for someone else once you are back in the light.[2]

At cool of day with God I walk, my garden's grateful shade; I hear his voice among the trees, and I am not afraid.

CHAPTER SIX

WE LONG TO BELONG

How the cattle moan!
The herds mill about
because they have no pasture.
                                        —Joel 1:18

I ALWAYS CRINGE at phone calls late at night. But this time it wasn't the sheriff with a report on my wayward daughter, it was Ginger.

"I can't go to this wedding. I just can't," she uttered in a desperate voice.

"Calm down, tell me all about it."

The invitation came that afternoon from a childhood friend, a recent widow who'd found a special man. It only reminded Ginger how she'd been forsaken by her own. After we talked it out for a while she asked, "Why can't I get control over my emotions?"

"You will, later. Just flow with them right now."

"I just want a man's arms around me. You tell me to make God my husband. I'm trying. Trying to pray to Him for support and for all the things a husband is supposed to do, but it's not working, Jan. I feel like a leper, excluded from society, trapped in this house. I'm sick of it. I'm going crazy."

"I know, crazy is OK."

"Jeanne mentioned I might want to go to the Christian singles New Year's dance with you two, and I told her I'd think it over. Well, I've thought. I'm going!"

I was certain I heard Carly crooning in the background, "Haven't got time" for the *you know what.*

Ginger's ricochet of feelings was no surprise, but I needed some hot tea. "Hold on just a sec. Be right back." I groped around the kitchen for something to crunch on.

I came back on the line with some chamomile tea and silently promised to give Jeanne, my speak-before-she-thinks-friend, a few thoughts of my own in the morning.

"Jeanne mentioned the dance, eh?"

"I'll be safe with you two," Ginger insisted. "Don't worry."

That'll be the day. A gorgeous, vulnerable, touch-hungry redhead in a room full of music and males? Doubtful, even if we leashed her to us all night. Obviously, she hadn't heard my subtle warning about jumping into the singles pool too soon.

Wrapped in my terrycloth robe, I curled up in my La-Z-Boy recliner with charred cinnamon toast and started telling Ginger more harrowing stories—some real page-turners guaranteed to keep us both awake for a while.

I had breezed through Natalie's wedding like a trooper but afterwards unraveled like a fake Persian rug. Now what? My comrade was leaving me. Work had become a place of mending as two friends helped each other close the gaping holes in our hearts. I milled about in a room of desks, phones, and file cabinets, writing papers on California water and timber issues, working on casework. Tasks I enjoyed. Yet I missed my pal.

I finally decided to move off the hill and into a small duplex in town; I'd let go of the ranch, my country dream, and moved into a new phase of my life.

It was time.

Wondering where to begin with the boxes and clutter and my whole confusing life, I turned around to see a petite woman with a plate of warm brownies arrive at the door and welcome me to the neighborhood.

Jeanne made her entrance into my life.

It's the friends we can call up at 4 a.m. that matter.
—Marlene Dietrich

Just when God swept Natalie away to her "Promised Land," just when I questioned if I would ever belong anywhere, along came Jeanne. She couldn't have been more different than my gardening friend. Jeanne was perky, talkative, optimistic, always on the move. After six years of marriage to her college sweetheart and two children, the dream of a happy family dissolved. When we met, she was separated from her second husband, Tom.

"Within a short time of my marriage crumbling, I found another love. He was so much fun," she told me soon after we met. "Fabulous dancer. He taught me golf and fishing and played with my kids. As a Catholic, I felt awkward moving in with him and guilty about our relationship, so we got married." During the twelve years she discovered Tom had lied to her about almost everything, including a nonexistent cancer that he cleverly used to manipulate her.

Not to mention several ex-wives lurking in his past.

Still she followed her restless husband to a small California mountain town where he drove a logging truck, hoping that the friendly, quaint environment could settle him down at last. But Tom had a wanderlust and left home for months at a time.

Her neighbor Susan began to share with her about the deep things of God, things Jeanne had never heard of in Catholic school. Soon she began attending an evangelical, Bible teaching church and found a true relationship with the living God, so different from the ritual of worship of her childhood. "Then I began to pray for love for Tom, and God gave it to me. He gave me peace to live in the chaotic situation."

When she and I first became friends, Tom had been gone for a year and a half, and Jeanne wondered what to do. He didn't want to be married any longer. While she had no intention of seeking another husband, she felt undefined, neither single nor married. As we walked the neighborhood every morning before work, we shared our personal prayer requests.

"I'm wondering," she mentioned casually one day, "is there a way to search marriage records in California? I figured you might know from your work down at the Capitol. There's some information I'd like to find."

My ears pricked at the suggestion. "Just call me Ms. Super Sleuth. Your wish is my command. What do you need?" Of all my tasks on the job, researching ranked as the most fun. It satisfied all my needs to pry and snoop.

After a week at making inquiries, I'd found more than I bargained for. "Jeanne, are you sitting down? Tom was never divorced from wife number three."

"What! Are you sure?"

Tom and the marriage were both a fraud.

Meanwhile his emphysema was killing him, and Tom, in desperation, committed suicide rather than suffer a painful death. After the funeral Jeanne's dammed-up emotions all gushed out; she let go all the hurt she'd stored up while holding together the first family and all the strain of trying to make the second marriage work. Being no stranger to grieving, I joined her, praying and crying with my new friend as we both repented over our mistakes.

Through Jeanne's example I began to get a glimpse of godly grief. "For consider how much diligence . . . this grieving as God wills—has produced in you: what a desire to clear yourselves, what indignation, what fear, what deep longing" (2 Cor. 7:11).

So far my sorrows had come from my personal losses with little thought to how my actions may have grieved my heavenly

Father. Through Jeanne, I finally understood His love for me, the tears He shed because I went astray.

Sorrow hit me full in the face. Together Jeanne and I repented over our impure relationships and their consequences, and from then on we were bonded.

If you can't be a good example, then just be a horrible warning.
—Catherine Aird

"Jeanne will tell you," I cautioned Ginger between bites of toast, "that she rushed into that relationship on the rebound. She didn't see any of the signs because this man made her feel so good, took her dancing, made her laugh. She fell in love with the way he made her feel about herself."

Ginger cleared her throat. "I'm not looking for a man."

I clenched my teeth. Ouch. Had it not sunk in about Jeanne's regrets over rushing into a marriage with Tom? She had obviously forgotten what she had said a few moments before: *"I just want a man's arms around me."*

Selective listening. We're all so good at it.

"We are never looking," I said flatly. "We're just scanning the aisles for an antidote for the pain, and we run into a diversion."

I settled in my chair, pulled the afghan up around my neck and started in on Susan's story. Another locust lesson.

Shortly after meeting Jeanne, she asked me to go with her to Bakersfield during Easter break to visit her dear friend and spiritual mentor. During the five-hour drive I heard a tale that sounded more like a soap opera thriller than reality. It grew more bizarre with every mile and made my own odyssey seem like just an embarrassing B movie.

Then I met her, a fragmented woman, still in emotional disrepair, staggering in the wake of disastrous choices after personal tragedy. Susan was not shy to talk about it, actually eager to do so. Raised in an alcoholic home full of secrets and fears, Susan learned early on how to avoid conflict, how to take care of everybody to keep the peace whenever possible. Like all her siblings, she married to get out of the house and ended up more miserable.

"Paul controlled me—where I could go, what I could buy." Yet she worked hard to please him, their two daughters and a son. "I danced everybody else's dance," she told me. "I lived my life for everyone else, and it took its toll."

At twenty-seven, the birth of her third child triggered a breakdown. "I took prescription drugs and tranquilizers rather than end up in a psyche ward." But she did end up in counseling where she realized that she was unraveling. All the suppressed trauma she'd suffered as a child couldn't stay buried forever.

Growing up, she had a deep faith and had gone to mass faithfully but never experienced the love or power of God in her life. Now she yearned for it, and she found a group of charismatic Catholics. Soon she began attending Bible studies. Seeing the change in Susan, Paul's curiosity led him to accompany her. Soon he embraced the Lord. As the couple found friendships with other Christians, Paul became "on fire for God," as Susan describes. A man with no prior interest in religion, Paul was now on a spiritual high, she told me, inviting everyone he met to taste the fruit of God's love.

After eighteen years of marriage, she thought, we're going to live happily ever after as a family!

But a year later Paul was diagnosed with cancer and died six months later. "It happened so fast. He was in and out of the hospital but had a regular ministry telling people how he was ready to go home and be with Jesus. People were being saved right and left. He was witnessing on the day he died."

Fully confident that she had prepared for his death, Susan donned her tough and strong suit, stifled her grief, and clung to her self-sufficiency. There was one serious flaw in her plan, though; she avoided discussing their father's death with her children, nor did she ask what they were feeling along the way.

She assumed they'd see her example and bounce back.

A year later the elastic snapped, and the children were a mess. Maybe Joe, the youth pastor and worship leader of their church could help, she thought. Maybe he would have some suggestions on what to do with her three acting-out teenagers.

"He was our rescuer. He drew us into his life and family," she says. "He was always counseling with the children and helping me, especially with Clint acting out his anger. We had prayer meetings at their house. He made us feel like we belonged somewhere."

She had no clue as to how the devil planned to blindside her, taking hostage the spiritual crop planted before Paul's illness. He's the great hijacker and waits for the chance to exploit our weakness, to take us as "POWs"—Prisoners of Woe.

You showed me how, how to leave myself behind
How to turn down the noise in my mind
Now I haven't got time for the pain.
                                        —Carly Simon

A romance with Joe, a married pastor, never crossed her mind. "It was the friendship with a godly man who seemed so wise that enticed me ever so subtly."

Joe had a dream of starting his own church, purchasing an established center for a ministry base, and Susan caught his vision, even accompanying him on a search down to Southern California. They found the perfect spot, ten acres with five homes, "where we could all live together," Joe announced.

It seemed to Susan an ideal situation, a family ministry where they would all live happily together and serve the Lord. Despite her reservations she agreed to invest everything, all the money she had, to help purchase the property. On the way home Joe suggested they stop and get a beer.

"I was so naive. It never occurred to me that a man of the church couldn't be trusted. After two drinks I succumbed to my loneliness. Felt free and loose as the wind. In a flash I was caught up in a full-blown affair."

Oops.

His marriage and ministry didn't detour this man from pursuing her. Once they moved to the ranch to start the ministry, she told herself, it would all go away; they would stop. "Yet we carried on for years, secretly. I never realized my neediness. I blocked out my guilt and sin against God. It just felt so good to be desired. I suppose it's what they mean by 'addicted to love.'"

For eight years her daughters never knew the truth. Her son finally stormed off angrily one night and never came home.

The sorrow over her son and shame over her secret affair with Joe took its toll. Finally, like the dry rot under a deck that eventually collapses the entire structure, the emotional fungus couldn't be ignored. She dredged up the courage to break it off and to leave the church, and then Susan limped into counseling.

A secret is the only thing that circulates faster than money.

One day her daughter called feverishly. "Mom! The word is that Joe has committed adultery. You know everything that goes on in this church. Who was it?"

Imagine having to admit to your daughter that you are the woman described in Proverbs 5:3! "For the lips of an adulteress drip honey, and her speech is smoother than oil; but in the end she is bitter as gall."

Her daughters were furious at her confession. They wanted her to come forward to expose Joe and see him punished, but Susan hadn't the strength to face the ordeal.

All the suppressed anger and pain of their childhood losses spewed out at their mother. With hotheads and cold hearts, they shut her out of their lives.

Susan's hope vanished. In 1990, she found herself in a Christian psychiatric hospital in Southern California. "I was an emotional cripple. I couldn't work. I didn't care if I ever did anything for God again. How could He ever use me now that I'd made such a mess?"

It took the guidance of professionals and a long time of soul-searching for her to understand the force of God's grace. Along with the promise in Joel, Susan took comfort in Isaiah 42:3: "A bruised reed he will not break, and a smoldering wick he will not snuff out."

When we're weak and defenseless, even if we've botched it up ourselves, God will be tender to those who call out. When the lamp wick that burns with zeal in the beginning starts to flicker and dim, He'll cup hands around it to keep it faintly lit until it can glow again.

"God used this time to clean me up," Susan says. "I had the zeal but not the wisdom to keep from being deceived."

The temptation was subtle, drawing her into an illicit affair because, like most of us, she longed to belong. The seeds of faith, sprouted before her husband's illness, were weak and defenseless after her loss. Instead of seeking God Himself, she sought a neutralizer for the pain.

To embrace the pain doesn't mean we have to enjoy it
but be willing for God to use it as a tool to change us.

Back to my late-night telephone conversation with Ginger—in the wee hours of that morning I assured her, "I'm not telling you this because I fear you might go the same way. Susan's story is pretty extreme, but none of us are exempt from the great hijacker, the devil, who will try anything to steer us off course."

Stillness for a moment. Ginger mulled over everything I'd just told her. "Please tell me this grim story has a good ending."

"Absolutely. It's amazing what God does when we surrender. I'll tell you the rest of it later, I promise. It's too late now, OK?" I held back a yawn and stretched my neck and shoulders to keep from getting stiffer.

What I hoped Ginger would glean from these stories is our universal need as women to belong, to someone or something. When we face any kind of loss, we lose our membership in a cherished club, one that gave us identity and purpose. Sitting outside the life we knew so well, waiting on the healing process, feeling no purpose and no direction, is frustrating.

But we're hampered by our unwillingness to wait on God only, by our bouts of unbelief. Will He really do what He promises to do?

When our hopes grow dim, we always tend to look for an alternate light source. But be careful; when we dull the edges of our pain by chasing new activities, new scenery, new friends or lovers, the scars are still there, not permanently closed. They're tender and hidden, waiting to burst open down the line. Joining clubs and singles groups, taking classes, or pursuing new ministry adventures are each helpful, but they're only Band-Aids, temporary cover-ups for the real healing work that needs to occur.

Been there, done that. I tried to keep Ginger from the mistaken thinking that any new person or activity would ease her problems.

"Jan, I want to do this right, I do, but how? I'm so weary, so confused."

And ripe for stepping in harm's way.

"God will do this if you're willing. It made all the difference for Susan. That's why she has a new, more profitable life than ever before."

Sudden silence from Ginger on the other line. I was reminded of what my friend and nationally known speaker Florence Littauer said in a seminar once, "Are you willing? OK, are you willing to be willing? Start there."

Florence understands loss. She had two sons with severe brain damage.

It's a bit scary to face the unknown, to enter into a covenant with God as your Maker, your husband. Yet God thinks about you as His bride, and your name is on His lips. He knows your need to belong and has made the way.

Because God is God we have carte blanche with our lives, a green light to respond to our circumstances in whatever way we choose.

What will you choose?

Oswald Chambers writes that we must *will to obey*. When God gives a vision of truth, it's never a question of what He will do, but of what we will do.[1]

So what'll it be for you? Are you willing to take His outstretched hand to lead you from the darkness? Are you willing to be willing?

Good. You're on your way.

CHAPTER SEVEN

WASH YOUR HANDS AND
THROW IN THE TOWEL

Declare a holy fast.
—Joel 2:15

GINGER STAYED HOME on New Year's Eve, so the year came in with a bubble instead of a bang, but hurrah! She had symbolically crossed the Maginot Line, that string of fortifications, minefields, and encampments placed at the border by the French but later overrun by the Germans during World War II. Once the good guys, the Allies, broke through the line after the D-Day invasion, there was no turning back.

It was an all-out push for victory.

If we could sell our experiences for what they cost us
we'd be millionaires.
—Abigail Van Buren

After the holidays, we started our Monday night women's Bible study at my house, and Ginger took up residence in one of the empty chairs. Our topic—the book of Ruth; our theme—obedience and surrender.

Not exactly a ladies' tea party, but we all agreed we were ready to tackle it, even Ginger. On week two she came with her Bible, a pile of notes, and a woman she'd met at church.

Claudia came in search of a group of women who "aren't afraid to be honest about their struggles."

Struggles? We had a bonanza of them, and honesty? We got pretty adept at looking painful truths in the face.

A registered nurse in her forties, Claudia was emerging from her second divorce. "I married young the first time for fear of getting sexually involved," she said, not mincing any words. During this difficult marriage, which included three daughters, Claudia grew convinced of her need for a closer walk with God. "I learned God was my true husband and would always be there for me no matter what. He was the only one who could change me into a godly wife and mother, the only one who could deal with my husband's addiction to women and alcohol."

After eighteen years her commercial pilot husband said he was tired of trying to walk the Christian walk. He packed his bags and moved out of state.

"I was devastated, and it took a long time to get on with my life. I couldn't even think about dating. I was pretty disillusioned with men, plus all the rules of relationships seemed to be different. I asked myself, 'How do two people spend time together and not cross the boundaries?' When I posed the question to girlfriends, their answer was, 'Impossible, why try?' Satan's lies took hold of my thinking at that point."

A few years later a coworker encouraged her to go on a blind date. "There were no bells, but he was a believer, I thought. As our relationship progressed to a more serious level, the same old problem came up: Did God's Word regarding sexual immorality really apply to adults in the twentieth century? The man I was dating didn't believe it did. OK, that should have been a 'red flag,' but I bought it. After all, I'd been celibate for years, and surely God would be forgiving, right?"

So the boundaries were crossed. "Satan is so cunning. I decided to enjoy this time of pleasure, of feeling desired. When

Satan gets a foothold, he doesn't give up. My sin kept me estranged from God."

After fifteen months they married. "I knew right away we were in deep trouble. We agreed on very little, especially the Christian life. In the end he was drawn to New Age thinking, and the marriage ended before three years. How hard it was to face this mistake. I wasn't even on the rebound. What a fool."

To add to her desolation and feelings of failure, the doctors discovered advanced degenerative arthritis that required a total hip replacement. "As a nurse, this caught me off guard! What rotten timing! What was God doing?"

Off work for five months, Claudia spent hours on end in prayer and retrospective thinking. "I came to see God's timing as a blessing. It was during this period that I asked God to bring into my life strong, committed Christian women who were not afraid to discuss difficult topics. Ginger says this is the place to be, so here I am!"

I flashed Ginger a "thumbs-up" sign. (Proud of you, girl!)

"The only single women I know," Claudia continued, "aren't denying themselves pleasures of the flesh, and they call themselves Christians! So tell me—how do you ladies live without sex?"

No whitewashing over things with Claudia. Oh, boy. Any pat answers out there, anyone? You could hear the simultaneous snapping of workbooks being set down on the oak coffee table. Cancel the study, it's a sober-truth night.

A frank talk is good soap for the hearts.
—Arabian Proverb

Julie offered her story first, and as she spoke, her words took me back a few years, to a time that tried a friendship.

I met cute, dark-haired Julie while out "jogging" in my new neighborhood. Or rather, she jogged—I shuffled my feet swiftly. We soon became power-walking pals, Julie, Jeanne, and me. Married twice, once briefly just out of high school,

Julie had been through some rough years full of hurt and regret but was now raising two young sons and trying to be a faithful Christian. We soon found a single fellowship group in a nearby town and were off to swim parties, family barbecues, hikes, and countless activities, all centered around the Lord. All harmless fun.

Until the country dance lessons.

Julie discovered her passion. "It's all harmless," she assured me when she signed up for advanced lessons at a local country western club. "Why don't you give it a try? It's so much fun." I shook my head. Dancing had already gotten me into trouble enough for one lifetime.

We began to see Julie less and less. Three nights a week she frequented the club, entering dance competitions and winning a great many. Her dancing buddy, whom I'll call Roy, was a successful attorney, an outstanding dancer, and extremely nice—but married. "Dancing doesn't interest his wife, and she doesn't mind, really. I've met her, and she seems nice."

Excuse me? Whirling around in my head were visions of Bob handing over a line like that when he stepped out on me. "Julie, be careful," I cautioned. In other words, jump ship now!

Girl overboard! Mayday! Mayday!

"Help! I'm falling for him," she confessed a few months later. We sat on her bed gabbing like two teenagers while I begged her to hang up her dancing shoes for a while. Yes, yes, she agreed it was the only way.

No, she couldn't bring herself to do it. So Roy left his wife and children to become half of a dancing duo with Julie, and as they waited for his divorce to come through, they planned a Lake Tahoe wedding.

She and I had one last tearful talk one sultry summer night by the Doughboy pool in her backyard. "I know you love me, Jan, and I know what I'm doing isn't right, but I can't give him up. Please understand."

In the corner of my mind, I could almost hear the faint, muffled snore of slumbering locusts lying in wait.

How well I understood that urgent yearning of the flesh! Yet I feared for my sweet friend and what the future would bring. Along with her dance trophies came an unforeseen consolation prize—Roy's ex-wife suddenly died of pneumonia, and his five girls moved in. Her dancing days were numbered.

And so was the marriage. For years Julie tried to hang on, to make it work, and as she turned back to the Lord for comfort and guidance, things only got worse.

The dance of pleasure was now the dance of pain.

"It was a long ride after Roy divorced me," she said. "A runaway roller coaster, especially when he wouldn't let me go, wanted to see me all the time. I couldn't give him up, either. It was craziness. Thankfully, these ladies kept praying for me, that I'd realize I needed the Lord more than a man, that I would desire Him instead of the needs of the flesh. It's so powerful, though—know what I mean?"

Nods in unison. Then one by one we gave snippets of our own stories, of indulging our love hunger, dining with the wrong people in the wrong places. By the end of the night, Claudia joined our little bridal party as we groomed for our Prince Charming, our Kinsman Redeemer, The Prince of Peace.

BAD FOR A SEASON, BUT NOT FOREVER

Few of us make it an ambition to be a bad girl, says author Liz Curtis Higgs. "Badness" can be falling short in any way, a temporary condition that isolates us from God.

Maybe you grew up in a "good-girl home" like she did. "Nice town, nice parents, all the right friends, all the right activities. But when I hit my mid-teens and the '70s rolled around, suddenly that charming small town became stifling. The honor society pals were nerds." She threw caution—and everything else—to the wind and pursued a party lifestyle with gusto for a full decade. "When the world went crazy with drugs, sex and rock 'n' roll, I was wide-eyed and ready for the ride."

"It got so much worse before it got better," she admits in her book, *Bad Girls of the Bible, and What We Can Learn from Them.* "Only a few trusted souls on this earth know how bad. Jesus knows. He knows every inch of my heart. He knows how bad I was, am now and will be, before I leave behind this transient shell and go on to undeserved glory."[1]

She wants to share some good news: *He loves us anyway.*

"He loves us so much He will put people in our paths to lead us to Him, just as He did for me." Liz spent ten years in what she calls the "wanton wilderness" looking for joy, and she settled for fun, the kind that came in a bottle, a pill, or the arms of a stranger. She discovered a sad truth: fun and joy are not the same thing after all.

"Such fun is temporary at best; it's risky and even dangerous at worst. Not to mention, breaking the heart of the One who made us in His image."

"Oh, girlfriend," she writes, "When I think of the shallow relationships, the misspent dollars, the wasted years, I can taste that bitter despair all over again. I was a woman without hope—a bad girl by choice and by circumstances, convinced that if I just found the right man, he would save me from my sorrows."

Meanwhile some new Christians she'd met were full of joy about the Lord who loved her just as she was. Like my 3-D group, Liz's friends never pointed out that she was a "bad girl" or told her to "clean up her act." They loved and didn't judge, exactly what Scripture tells us to do.

One wintry day in 1982, when Liz was twenty-seven, she met the "right man"—who willingly had given His life to set her free. "Me. Sinful, disobedient, rebellious, me! Finally, I understood the depth of my badness and the breadth of God's goodness and so embraced His gift of grace with both hands."

After reading her book, I asked Liz, "What made you finally accept the offer of salvation?"

"Only the Lord Himself could answer that one," she replied.

"I think because I had tried all the world had to offer, and I knew what an empty, shallow existence it was. I'm a slow learner. It would be much wiser to accept someone else's word for the truth and skip all the bad girl stuff. But when you are a rebel, when you have a stubborn streak as wide as the sky, then you have to learn the hard way."

Can you relate? I'm nodding right now.

Her process from bad girl to redeemed girl was the easiest decision Liz ever made. Her surrender was total, 110 percent. "I never do anything halfway." So the Lord did all the work.

There are some minor details being worked out, she admits, and she's still a sinner saved by grace. "But, oh that saved part! What a glory! No one could be less worthy than me."

Three years after meeting up with the Lord, enjoying her life as a single woman, she met Bill. From the moment she laid eyes on him, she observed something special about the man she has now been married to for over fifteen years. Bill is the director of operations for her busy speaking and writing ministry. Aside from dozens of books, Liz chats up a storm on radio and television and speaks at retreats and events all over the country.

"It has taken me most of my Christian life to realize," she added, "that what I used to think of as my wasted years, my lost years, my locust years, are in fact, the heartbeat of my ministry today. Without my past I would not have this calling. I would surely have some calling, but not this one, this passion for reaching women who are languishing in a deep, dark pit— this could only come from God and from those years I spent dwelling in the pit myself."

When she speaks publicly, Liz shoots straight from the hip, not trying to make her story pretty, because "it wasn't." Sometimes she watches as some of the women in the audience pull back emotionally, even physically, at her candid account of her before-Christ life. The room grows very quiet, and women's eyes reveal their thoughts: "Oh, you were *that* kind of woman."

"Women who've grown up in the church don't always know what to do with the bad girls, even the redeemed ones," she says. "And there are thousands of us. As I share my own story, women track me down and pour their hearts out." She hears comments like, "No one in my church knows, I can't tell a soul, I always thought I was the only one."

No way, baby. Our Monday night Bible study can attest to that.

Liz can finally say, "Thank you, Lord, not only for rescuing me from that pit but for *leaving* me down there for a decade and sparing my life that I might give it to you completely."

Her life verse is 1 Timothy 1:15–16, which reads: "Christ Jesus came into the world to save sinners—and I am the worst of them. But I received mercy because of this, so that in me, the worst of them, Christ Jesus might demonstrate the utmost patience as an example to those who would believe in Him for eternal life."

> *Our past doesn't determine our future.*
> · —Liz Curtis Higgs

Let's review the climate of the times in the book of Joel. Wicked Queen Athaliah seized power in a bloody coup but was overthrown a few years later. Then Joash was crowned king, but since he was a wee seven years old, he needed some spiritual guidance. In those early years he did follow God but soon turned away and did his own thing.

And the people followed suit. They forgot about God.

Bring on Joel and his call to the people to turn back to their maker. "Declare a holy fast; call a sacred assembly" (Joel 1:15).

A day of wrath is coming, he warns, God's wrath against all evil. Not just the Gentiles, either. We're talking everybody, the whole enchilada, the nation of Judah too. This time the outbreak would be much worse than you've ever seen. Yet, Joel explains, it is a day that can be a blessing for God's people *if they repent.*

So declare that holy fast and hurry up about it, he pled.

Have you ever fasted? I always considered a fast a time to lay off food for a while in order to pray diligently about something important. Digging deeper into the issue, I find that the early Hebrews were in the habit of fasting whenever they were in trying circumstances, whether they were facing loss or merely tiptoeing into sin. The mere thought of a fast implied a sacrifice of the personal will.

It's the sacrifice that gives fasting its value.

At different times each of us in the Bible study group had repented of our mistakes and wrong attitudes (remember the godly sorrow we talked about earlier?) and mended our ways. We turned over a new leaf, reformed, walked the straight and narrow, put on sackcloth and ashes—however you choose to describe it. We made decisions to quit chasing after counterfeit ways to fulfill us as women.

We declared a holy fast.

God had brought each one of us to a place where we wanted to honor Him and where we had agreed to surrender our desire for intimacy with a man.

We never denied the yearnings; that's a big mistake. It only gives them more hidden power.

Paul hinted at this when he wrote, "You took off your former way of life, the old man that is corrupted by deceitful desires; you are being renewed in the spirit of your minds; you put on the new man, the one created according to God's likeness in righteousness and purity of the truth" (Eph. 4:22).

And here's the banner for us, "Since you put away lying, 'speak the truth, each one to his neighbor,' because we are members of one another" (Eph. 4:25).

So what good does it do to pretend we're above temptation, even if we're out of the sin?

"I have promised you in marriage to one husband—to present a pure virgin to Christ. But I fear that, as the serpent deceived Eve with his cunning, your minds may be corrupted from a complete and pure devotion to Christ" (2 Cor. 11:2–3).

Something is always trying to lead us astray.

After my struggle in breaking off an impure relationship, I asked God to teach me how to rechannel the emotional and physical energy that a sexual relationship expended. I was still young, facing a future without a man, at least in the short term and maybe forever, a fact in itself that tempted major resistance to the holy Christian life.

I felt gypped in my marriage, and I longed to experience a God-honoring one.

The million-dollar question I had to ask myself: If I never experience biblical love between a man and a woman, can I trust God and serve Him anyway for the rest of my life?

What is your question? It may begin like one of these: If I can never experience the joy of motherhood, . . . If I lose my precious loved one, . . . If this illness won't go away, . . . can I trust God and serve Him anyway for the rest of my life?

I wish I had a snappy comeback answer—"Of course I can, Lord," but to *put away lying,* I must admit my struggle. Knowing me, God expected this spiritual slugfest. To struggle and then yield means that the decision to walk with God will be a total one.

A forever pledge. An unretracted oath. One that will go the distance.

God cannot restore you unless you'll let Him wash your stains. What that means for you, I can't say. What you must surrender, I don't know, but God does. It may be a sexual relationship or impure thoughts or regret or bitterness or a pessimistic spirit. If you're not sure, ask Him, and He'll reveal it to you.

In Joel 2:12–13a, God declares, "Return to me with all your heart, with fasting and weeping and mourning. Rend your heart and not your garments."

In ancient days it was customary to show grief by tearing one's clothing while at the same time weeping loudly. While it's still good to shed the tears, express the sorrow and shame, and wear all the other stripes for the bumbles we've made, these actions are not enough to please the Lord. It's too easy simply to confess it all, and we can fool ourselves into thinking we're going to try a better way now. But God is a wise Father. We are His daughters, but He wants us to be first-rate.

He wants our complete hearts.

The verse continues, "For he is gracious and compassionate, slow to anger and abounding in love, and he relents from sending calamity. Who knows? He may turn and have pity and leave behind a blessing."

Special favors for His children.

Finally, after detailed sketches describing the destruction to the land by the locusts, we see the glimmer of hope. Here is the emotional response we've been waiting for—God's mercy and compassion ready to spill over.

His character revealed. He is ready to respond with grace, even when we don't deserve it.

As she met with us weekly, Claudia began to heal as a woman. "I began to see my womanhood as a valuable gift. I will never forget the story we read about a young man who fell in love with a beautiful antique and saved many months before he could purchase this item. He would stop by the store to gaze at this heirloom and make plans to care for it once it was his. In the meantime the storekeeper watched over his treasure. I learned that God is capable of being the storekeeper of my heart and womanhood if I surrender to His loving care."

The day I declared my holy fast, I'd been reading Florence Littauer's *Silver Boxes: The Gift of Encouragement,* in which she suggests that our words should be gifts to one another, like silver boxes with bows on top.[2] Instantly I saw myself as a bride with a gift for my husband, my Maker, a little silver box with a pledge of my love. Not a gift certificate to be redeemed later, but a gift for this day, this moment.

Wrapping an empty shoebox with silver paper, I attached a shiny ribbon and set it on my dresser: *This is my sacrifice to you, Lord—my sexual desires.*

By this time in my career, my salary allowed me extra money to give to my favorite ministries. Money would not be a real sacrifice for me, but *this* certainly would. It was the one thing I yearned for in the dark stillness of the night—the tender transfer of sexual love.

The sight of that box every evening when I slipped on my nightie made my heart swell. How precious a gift for my Lord! It was something as valuable to me as the alabaster jar of expensive perfume Mary of Bethany poured on Jesus' head before the last supper. The precious ointment of her affection.

He said she had done a *beautiful thing.*

What a sense of happiness filled me! The box symbolized my heartfelt vow to the Lord.

When I accepted Him into my life, He gave me absolute holiness as a wedding gift, but until I completely dedicated myself to leading an unstained life, His work of making me a righteous woman could not truly begin.

The silver box on my dresser reminded me of a union so pure and strong that when I was tempted later on (yes, yes, oh, yes!) it whispered promises to me much sweeter than the wishes of a fickle heart.

CHAPTER EIGHT

CALLING OUT

To you, O Lord, I call.

—Joel 1:19

AS SHE HUDDLED beside the emergency room hallway window, Linda covered her eyes with her hands and tried to block the horror of the afternoon. The scene whirled through her thoughts; eighteen-month-old Laura snuggled in her car seat— the red taillights reflecting on the damp pavement in front of her. "My foot reached for the brakes. When I tried to slow the car, it spun violently out of control. Then the thunderous explosion of metal roared in my ears as my body strained against the seat belt. We hit a minivan almost head-on. I couldn't believe I was still alive. The silence that followed chilled my heart. Why, why wasn't my baby crying?"

She turned to the back seat, and instead of seeing Laura's frightened, blue-gray eyes, she stared into a jagged empty hole. She clawed her way out of the wreckage and found Laura, still strapped in her car seat in the middle of the freeway, bleeding from one ear. "I knelt in the mud and pleaded with God for her life."

Laura had a fractured skull, and the doctor said, "We're sorry, but she will never awaken. She's in a vegetative state." A vegetable? No, she was a little girl held captive by her body.

"Looking at my sleeping beauty," Linda said, "I constantly cried, *How much longer, God?*"

Days turned into months in a hospital in Denver. One evening a physician stood in the doorway of Laura's hospital room, listening to the mechanical breathing of her respirator. "He avoided my eyes as his words chilled the air. 'Linda, Laura is not going to recover. You might as well———'"

His unspoken words screamed, "End it now! Pull the plug!" He awaited her response. "I swallowed hard, knowing we were playing a dangerous game, a game Laura couldn't afford for me to lose. I wearily tried to hide in silence, wishing for the deadly moment to pass." Finally she found her voice. "But my daughter is not dead!"

She took a deep breath and clenched her fists. "Laura has too much brain activity! Besides, what makes you think she's not going to recover?"

The doctor led her into a nearby office. "You need to face facts. Half of Laura's brain has been destroyed."

"But half of her brain is intact. Are you telling me you can scientifically factor the impact of what my love, faith, and prayers will have on this child's future?"

The doctor grudgingly admitted, "No."

She pressed. "Then your prognosis is only a guess. You see, God can take Laura, if He decides that is best. He has my permission, but it is not my role to pull the plug."

The doctor sighed, realizing he was up against a determined mother. Laura would live. Later Linda leaned against the doorjamb in Laura's room, closed her eyes, and prayed. *This victory is won, but how many others are left to fight? Lord, please see me through. For my hope and my comfort are in You and You alone.*

As she sat in the stillness of Laura's hospital room, holding her hand, watching for signs of life, she looked at the child she had fought and prayed so hard to keep. *She's really in there, isn't she?*

Then doubt crept in. What if the doctors are right, and Laura never wakes up? Maybe He's abandoned us. Maybe He isn't going to answer my prayers. Who am I trying to fool? I need to face facts—Laura will never awaken. She'll live the rest of her life as a vegetable, hooked to life support.

Linda tried to stifle her despair, but Laura's respirator seemed to rhythmically mock, *"no-hope, no-hope, no-hope."*

Everything seemed so pointless. Laura would be better off if she was to die, Linda concluded. After all, I can't allow her to live in this suspended state of life, can I?

"By now I had adjusted to the fact that Laura's smile would never return. My dreams for her were dashed. And God? He had been as silent as Laura's stilled voice."

She was truly alone in that out-of-town hospital, miles from her husband, miles from Laura's awareness, and light-years from the God she had trusted. Perhaps His silence meant that she should take matters in her own hands and end this terrible suffering.

She thought, I can kill Laura without the doctor's help. I can turn off the alarms and unplug the respirator from the wall. It would be so simple, except, she wondered, if I kill my daughter, how can I live with myself? How can I face Paul or my parents?

She stared at a bottle of painkillers. If I swallow them, she thought, no one will find us until morning. Laura and I could escape this living hell together.

Just as her plan seemed like the only solution, she found her hand resting on her belly. She knew suddenly that an unborn child was there. Her mind cleared. How could she kill herself? And Laura? A new life had just started growing inside her, and it had a right to live.

Her perspective returned. *Lord, I'm willing to wait— despite the pain and the cost. I'm willing to wait on You.* The words of Isaiah 40:31 came into her consciousness: "They that wait upon the LORD shall renew their strength; they shall mount up with wings as eagles; they shall run and not be weary; and they shall walk and not faint" (KJV).

She cried herself to sleep, terrified of the murders she had almost committed.

Many of the therapists who worked with Laura simply gave up, and Linda was terrified to take her home. "But it was the best decision we ever made. Once home, our days were filled with nurses, the beeping of life support equipment and new therapists who were willing to work on a child who remained unresponsive."

Then Laura emerged from her coma just before her baby brother Jimmy was born. Although her eyes fluttered open, her gaze was fixed. She was paralyzed, but though she was diagnosed blind, her eyes began to focus again.

If her faith were only strong enough, would Laura have been healed? One rainy afternoon, she slipped into Laura's room, planning to spend the time with God. "After an hour of earnestly telling God how much I believed He would perform a miraculous healing, I watched Laura's eyelashes flutter and she fixed her gaze on the ceiling as if I weren't there. I hit a wall. Suddenly I knew that my three-year struggle to carefully craft my faith had been for nothing."

She had no more strength left to believe. She had fought with everything in her and had lost. Laura's never going to get better, she told herself. Later, in the darkness of her bedroom, curtains drawn against the cold drizzle, she realized, "My hope was lost, replaced with shattered dreams." *Lord,* she prayed, *are You there? I need You to speak to me, if You want me to continue in my hope. Please show me what to do.*

That evening in church the pastor's thundering voice dropped to a low rumble. "Have you lost hope? God wants you to look up. He is with you and will restore your hope in Him."

"I was stunned. The message was too immediate to be a coincidence. Maybe God is with me, I reasoned."

Linda began to see that she had missed God's truth by placing her faith, not in Him, but in herself. "I had spent all my energy trying to have faith in faith! I had been held captive by trusting myself instead of trusting God."

In the stillness of the garage that night, she turned off the engine of the car, laid her head against the steering wheel, and prayed, *Lord, I transfer all my faith from myself to You.* "In my mind's eye, I could see Jesus' loving face as I handed Him back the limp body of my daughter. *Lord, she is yours. I am going to trust you with her future. My faith in you no longer depends on her healing.*"

> "Though he slay me, yet will I trust in him."
> —Job 13:15 KJV

Wow. I get the same goose bumps writing this as when I first heard Linda's story. I asked Linda for permission to include this intimate story, told mostly in her own words, of her lesson in faith.[1]

When Joel wraps up the first chapter, we notice he builds to a climax with a vivid account of the total ruin by the insects. Then we see him cry, "To you, O LORD, I call." Nothing can help the struggling people except God alone. It wasn't enough for them to grieve for their losses; they had to cry out, they had to pray, and they had to transfer their faith in themselves to the Lord.

Just like Linda did in her garage that night.

Linda's honest crying out through the tragedy and through her dry time brought her a closer, more fulfilling relationship with God. He is faithful, she wants to tell you, even when you're up to your neck in hot water.

Though Laura has to sit in a wheelchair and doesn't have the ability to speak, she can communicate with tongue signals and is a happy teenager who enjoys life and goes to public school in a purple wheelchair. "I think the ten months she spent in a coma was the time she spent with Jesus," Linda says.

"She has a special calm about her, a joyousness that comes from having a special relationship with God."

Calling out to the Lord during her dark time changed everything for Linda. And because she was homebound with her handicapped daughter, she turned to writing and was led into a new career as an author. She's started a nonprofit radio show that features inspirational stories.

"I believe God not only sustained me through my ordeal, but He also has gifted me with hope and joy to share with others," she says.

That's how He works every time. Calamity reminds us of our total dependence on Him.

And while Linda still catches herself once in a while shedding a tear over the Laura she lost, she embraces the Laura who returned. "My memories, even the painful ones, are now precious to me."

Memories contain the pattern of our life's quilt. Some of them are dark memories, shrouded in pain, but if we try to escape them or throw them away, the quilt will have big gaps; it will never be complete. Even the dark ones, Linda says, enrich the quilted pattern they helped create.

CHAPTER NINE

ONE STITCH AT A TIME

Return to the LORD your God,
for he is gracious and compassionate,
slow to anger and abounding in love.
                                              —Joel 2:13

"I'VE DECIDED to wait out the storm," Ginger announced casually one Friday morning in March.

Oh, if she could only hear the sound of trumpets going off in my head.

"Mind you, I don't feel so good about this holding pattern," she continued, "especially on my weepy days, but I know God is trying to teach me something—something big— and I don't want to miss it."

"Giving up the deadlines?" I teased.

"Yes—no more deadlines. I'm on God's timetable now."

The more we kept meeting, the more Ginger grasped of God's promises. He makes them, faith believes them, hope anticipates them, and patience quietly waits for them.

It's all in His time.

She began to accept the way grief and discontent and anger come in swells, with emotions rising and falling like tidal waves. They are unpredictable and inconsistent. The oddest things set us off one day and not the next.

And it's OK.

In this case knowledge is power. Once you know how it all works, you can brace yourself for the onslaught like the folks in the coastal hurricane states who prepare before the storm even starts. They make certain they have all their supplies, with ample sandbags on hand when they know the big waves are near.

Have you heard the phrase "time heals all wounds?" Don't buy it. It's not true. Time alone brings no healing, but God does, and He uses time to trap us in the restoring process, much like the chrysalis or pupa state of a butterfly. Think of that velvety cocoon. Inside is a wormy, hairy creeper, who, in her former state, couldn't move fast enough to escape her enemies. So there she lies, patiently awaiting transformation in a dark and quiet place. Then, at the right time, she emerges as a slender-bodied, vivid creature who can now flutter above it all.

It's a pretty good trade off, don't you agree? From gooey to gorgeous? It's what God does with us if we don't fight the process. Lean back, suspend, and mend. Then, presto! Before you know it, a different view of life, a new awareness of the world and all its possibilities.

When next you see a butterfly, think of her as God's grace unfolding from the darkness after a long rest.

"Jan," Ginger said with twinkling eyes, "Any bets on how long my wait will be?"

It all depends on the circumstances, I explained, and on the personality type of the one who's waiting.

If you're an impatient sanguine personality like me who would rather find fun and affirmation than spend too much time soul-searching, you may find yourself on a few detours. If you're a choleric who likes instant answers like Jeanne, you could resist giving over control to God. If you're a melancholy, like Mary Gail, forever striving for perfection, you may get caught up in self-pity or false guilt and have difficulty accepting God's outstretched arms. And if you're a cautious phlegmatic, like Connie, who hesitates to rock boats, you may resist moving out of your comfort zone.

Isaiah reminds us, "They that wait upon the LORD shall renew their strength; they shall mount up with wings as eagles; they shall run and not be weary; they shall walk and not faint" (Isa. 40:31 KJV).

Waiting builds strength.

It's more than counting flowers on the wall, as the old song goes. It takes *courage* to live in patience, to wait on the Lord and look eagerly to what is coming.

Patient waiting is often the highest way of doing God's will.
—Jeremy Collier

"How long, God?" That's what Barbara Hilford cried out in her frustration. "How much of my life—and now my retirement years, do I owe my mother? All? Part? A little more? A lot more?"

When I posted a request in the CLASS (Christian Leaders Authors and Speakers Seminars) weekly e-mail update, I asked for responses from women who had gained comfort from the promise of Joel 2:25. Immediately, I heard from Barbara.

"Amazing how God brings people together! When I read the note about your upcoming book, I simply had to respond." For twelve years she has been caring for her mother, who has Parkinson's disease. "She's entirely dependent on us now," she says.

People ask how she does it all.

"I used to give a faint smile and chirp something about God not giving us more than we can handle, then I'd struggle like crazy inside. Mom is becoming more childlike, not happy at all, and I'm more housebound than I was when my own daughters were small. I love her, and my husband too, and I see how difficult this situation is for him. I ask God, when will my life— our lives—be our own again?"

Through her prayers God gave her the answer when he drew her to Joel 2:25 a few years ago. "It has become my mainstay verse, the promise I cling to and thank Him for every day.

He has assured me that He will restore the years that the locusts have eaten."

And life doesn't have to be put on hold while she cares for her mother, Barbara discovered. "He tells me, 'Be patient, Barbara, rest in My care, wait for My timing. The day will come when I will have something else for You to do for me. But right now, this is where I need you, where you can best serve Me.'"

How can she refuse this request? "OK, God, my times are in your hand," she prays. "Thank you that you know me best."

Recently, I heard from her by e-mail. She let me know she's finally hired some day help to give her a four-hour respite from caregiving. "You know what, Jan? With all this escalation of duties and 'locust devouring' of what little freedom I have, I have managed to find a peace and comfort, a sense of tightly encircling arms holding me up and nudging me forward each day. I sense a smile and a nod and a 'that's my girl.' I know I'm on the right track and my efforts and struggles to hang in there, to surmount those occasional slips into discouragement, are the fertilizer for the harvest ahead.

"I've come to realize that this cup I've been given, this path I'm on, is not just about me and my needs or my situation, but a time of growing and learning for everyone else who's a part of my life, as well."

Those quiet (and seemingly endless) tough times have a purpose. They lay the stepping stones to that doorway to new beginnings—God's waiting room, the gateway to wholeness.

All comes at the proper time to those who know how to wait.
—St. Vincent de Paul

Habakkuk, the perplexed prophet, asked this question, "How long, O LORD, must I call for help, but you do not listen?"

God had a godlike answer: "Watch . . . and be utterly amazed. I am going to do something in your days that even you would not believe, even if you were told" (Hab. 1:2, 5).

Something beyond description. That's exactly what happened with our dear Connie, yet another woman God led to our group. My heartstrings flutter every time I think about it.

There we were gathered on Monday nights at my house, a group of women excited about studying the book of Ruth, drinking in more of how God brings good out of hopeless situations.

We were just at the point at which Ruth, who chose to follow her mother-in-law to a new land, is now a poor widow with little hope of remarriage. She has to glean the fields every day for food. Every now and then she is invited to share a meal with her employer, Boaz, and some of the workers. When Naomi discovers this bit of trivia, what does she do? What any clever mother-in-law would do—she slips into her Carol Channing *Hello Dolly* matchmaker mode and sets a plan into action.

Boaz, you see, is a kinsman, a not-so-distant relative, and under Jewish law he has certain responsibilities toward down-and-out family members, including—and this thrilled Naomi—that of providing an heir to maintain the line of a deceased brother.

I won't go into the story here, but Ruth returns home to an anxious mom-in-law who offers the right prescription: "Wait my daughter, until you find out what happens."

Ruth has done everything in her power, everything possible to secure her future and bring about her dreams, and now it is time to sit tight and leave it to the Lord.

As we know, Boaz claims his bride, and Ruth receives the privilege of being an ancestor to the Messiah, the Redeemer of the world.

Talk about suspend and mend. This girl got more than an alteration, she got the "whole life lift!"

Yes, it's a marvelous love story, but that's not what's in it for you. How about this? Strength and success often come when you just sit still.

When you look at Bible stories, you'll see how God responds to the needs of His people. Ruth obeyed and then waited, and God honored her faithfulness. The people of Judah repented of their stubbornness, and God sent the locusts scattering. Far more than that, he restored their crops to abundance. He'll do the same for you.

Patience may be bitter, but its fruit is sweet.

This is the lesson that transformed Connie. One summer, this mild-tempered blond set up her tent in the site next to our singles group on our annual campout weekend in the Sierra Buttes. We motioned her over to join our campfire. When she discovered we were from Auburn, she exclaimed with wide eyes, "I just moved there! I've been praying to meet some single friends."

Divine appointment time again?

Naturally we told her all about our Saturday night fellowship, where we met, and what kind of programs and activities we offered. A program director for a community center, Connie was in her late thirties. She had seen the world and had experienced many exotic adventures and a few romances along the way but had never gotten around to getting married.

"I hope to, though. I would like a family," she told us.

During our group activities, hikes, rafting trips, and bike rides, she and Vern drifted together and struck up a friendship. A great guy, funny and smart, Vern made no secret that starting another family at his age was not in his plan.

We all adored Vern and would never think of having a get-together without him and his adorable wit, but we "Monday night girls" concurred that he was not the right match for our Connie. Still we didn't say much at first.

The friendship seemed comfortable for Connie, almost like a plaid flannel bathrobe on a cool fall eve, and the two enjoyed the same passion for the outdoors. We grew concerned with the way Connie reconciled herself to a stagnant relationship. One weekend, Jeanne and I felt the urge to whisk her to the mountains for the weekend. A serious girl chat and prayer time was in order.

We never came out and suggested she break it off with Vern, but we engineered the conversation in that direction. (Yes, of course we were doing you-know-what again for the Lord, but trust me—it was necessary.)

"He has made it clear he'll never want more children," she admitted. "I was just hoping that after a while he might . . . ," she said with a faint moistness welling up in her eyes, "we do get along so well. I can't imagine being without him."

Maybe we should go back to biting our tongues, I thought, *and let God fix this one.*

Several weeks later she announced to us, "If God has something better for me, I'll never know it, not as long as I hold on to Vern."

One soft tear glided slowly down her cheek as she spoke.

But it wasn't easy letting go of the comfy plaid flannel—the months marched on into another year. We just scratched our heads and kept praying—*Lord, can't you bring the right man for Connie? Let us see your miracle unfold.*

The rest of us in the group had been divorced. We had children and had finally come to the place of contentment with our singleness. Still, we were romantics, believing the right relationship could be out there. But if only one of us could have those romantic dreams fulfilled, we agreed in prayer, *Let it be Connie.*

Through our study, things eventually became clear to her. "God is more interested in who I become than what I have, marriage or children. I want to be a woman who honors Him."

Like Ruth, Connie laid her dream at the feet of her Redeemer and waited. For the first time since we'd met her years ago, she had a hunger for God's Word and flourished in her new awakening of her faith. She determined to make Him first in her life and relaxed, resting in the sovereignty of God, no matter what.

And she finally ended things with Vern. When she told us, we all cried. It was a two-hanky-box night, for sure.

Dear God, she's done the hard things. Bring about her dream, I prayed. And I kept my eye open for an eligible man for Connie.

But nothing happened.

About six months later at the end of our Bible study time, Connie spoke in her relaxed, quiet way. "I'm thinking—about adopting a child. From Romania. My sister just did. What do you think?"

Where did this come from? It took a moment to process.

"I'm past forty now, and I've . . . ," she began slowly, "wasted so many years on . . . Even if I do meet a man now, it's awfully late."

God's gifts never come late.

In asking the Lord to bring Connie a *family,* we'd never considered this option, but why not? From us Connie had seen firsthand the challenges of being a single mom. "I can do this," she said. I'm ready for a new future. Why not give a home to a child who is abandoned?"

Yes, why not? What a great idea.

· We volunteered as her cheerleaders, rooting her onward. But we had to keep our pompons primed for a long, long time.

Door after door closed. First the Ukraine, then Russia. She signed on with two private worldwide adoption organizations, placing money up front. She waited as groups traveled to Russia only to come back with one or two babies, the only ones available. Then, an area doctor with worldwide connections made a trip overseas to search for babies in orphanages, only to come home with the report that the local mafia had absconded with Connie's $4,000.

A year and a half passed and nothing happened, but we kept praying, asking for clarity from God. *Could it be that you have other plans for Connie, Lord? Show us confirmation.*

Then one night we came across what God told our friend, Habakkuk: "The vision will still happen at the appointed time. It hurries toward its goal. It won't be a lie. If it's delayed, wait for it. It will certainly happen. It won't be late" (Hab. 2:3 *God's Word*).

We waited with Connie in confidence, with a new understanding. One way God can test our faith is with a delayed promise.

> *Never think that God's delays are God's denials.*
> *Hold on; hold fast; hold out.*
> —George-Louis Leclerec de Buffon

Suddenly the news arrived in December of 1995. Another agency to which Connie applied reported that China adoptions had just reopened, and she could be traveling with them to Shanghai in less than three months to pick up a child.

"I can't get too excited yet," she told us, but we all sensed that this was it. Isn't God the God of impossible dreams?

When Connie came in that Monday night with a photo of her five-month-old baby girl, we all wept with joy. We were going to be "aunties" to little Sadie!

Connie had the picture copied and enlarged—one for her home, her office, her car, and one for each one of us. The whole time she was overseas, we kept praying. "I felt the prayer covering every day," she told us later. "I needed your prayers so desperately."

None of us knew how much.

When the American group of eight families arrived at the orphanage to visit their babies before going on to Cltangzhou to finish the paperwork, Connie's heart pounded in her chest. The baby brought to her arms did not match the photo she knew so well. "It wasn't my baby at all! Not the child I'd bonded with."

Connie being Connie, she would never stir the pot, and making a fuss with a foreign government might mean receiving no child at all. "My stomach was in knots," she told us later. "If I took this child, what would happen to the one meant for me?"

After the paperwork was completed, the group was on their way back to get the babies. Connie cried out to the Lord, "Give me peace." At once she felt the Lord saying to her, "Connie, you've waited so long; I've brought you this far, so trust me." Instantly, a calm enveloped her.

"At the orphanage they let us look in the nursery area. I walked in the third room and looked down in the bed. There she was, my baby, Sadie! I knew every inch of her face. But when I showed the caretaker the photo, she shook her head to say the baby was far too young."

The Lord nudged Connie to persist, even though the caretaker spoke no English. Connie laid the photo next to Sadie and motioned with her hands what she was trying to convey. Sadie, confined to a crib all of her life, weighed only eleven pounds and looked much younger than five months. After a few minutes of comparison, the woman's eyes lit up, and she nodded in agreement. The photo and the baby in question were indeed the same.

Somehow the caretaker convinced the orphanage officials, who stepped in to correct the mistake. Through interpreters Connie discovered she could claim her rightful child.

Is this God's doing or what?

Before Connie arrived home, we'd planned a shower to welcome Sadie. What a testimony to God's goodness, to the way He surprises us with blessings beyond our comprehension! Lorena wrote this poem and presented it framed and matted on blanket-stitch paper:

A Song for Sadie

Little precious Sadie
From a land so far away,
Your Mommy prayed so long for you
And journeyed many a day.

She fell in love with you at once
In fact, the moment that she heard
That you would soon belong to her.
She clung to every hopeful word.

And when, for just a moment,
The babe before her was not you,
She said, "There has been some mistake,
This is not the babe I knew."

You see, the love your Mommy carried
Had grown, while yet apart.
More than a baby in the picture
Already a child in her heart.

When she went back to get her baby
And found you in the crowd,
All the glory went to Jesus,
She thanked Him right out loud.

"This is my baby, Sadie,
She's the one God chose for me,"
And by the grace of God's own hand
You came home across the sea.

Little precious Sadie,
There will never be a doubt
That for your special Mommy
God especially picked you out.

When Sadie came home, so did Connie's dream of motherhood. All that patient waiting brought her close to the Lord and helped her depend on Him as never before.

Oliver Wendell Holmes has this to say about patience: "Take your needle my child, and work at your pattern; it will come out a rose by and by."

Life is like that. One stitch at a time sewn patiently, and the pattern will emerge as a perfect tapestry with no hint of the knots and snarls on the underside.

One thing that encourages us is the character of God. Knowing that He is "gracious and compassionate, slow to anger and abounding in love" (Joel 2:13) will comfort us. His character flows out of His deep love for us. Remember, God is eager to bless. That should motivate us to seek and wait for His best, shouldn't it?

Connie may never marry, but the blessings of motherhood have given her a joy she could never have imagined. She traded her dreams for God's, and it made all the difference. A few years after Sadie came home, Mom and daughter began to pray for a sister, and baby Megan joined them from Linchuan, China, a year and a half later. Connie credits God for everything. She's dedicated herself to raising up her girls to know and love their Lord.

When your trust is fixed on God, you spirit clings to Him, and the waiting can be sweet.

CHAPTER TEN

VINEYARDS RETURNED

I am sending you grain, new wine and oil,
enough to satisfy you fully.
—Joel 2:19

LIFE WAS SIMPLE for Lisa, growing up in a small town in Iowa in the fifties and sixties. With seven brothers and sisters, she had the happy freedom to roam around all day, pedaling her bicycle for miles. From all appearances, hers was the perfect life, but this family had a dark side.

An abusive father.

"First he would go into my brothers' room," Lisa reveals; "then he would rush into my room screaming like a wounded animal. For what seemed like an eternity, he would punch me in the stomach and pull my hair. In the dizzying background I could hear my mother crying for him to stop."

She hated him with all the passion of a five-year-old girl.

When she grew up, Lisa's much older sisters assured her that she would find a true love and know the right man when he came along. Lisa loved children and longed to be a mother but shuddered at the thought of marriage and dealing with a man. In her late twenties she met one who swept her off her feet. He appeared to be sensitive, generous, and loving. Being educated in a military school had left him lonely, and he dreamed of a devoted wife.

His dream came true, and so did her nightmare. On the wedding night she witnessed his first outburst of anger and learned that he was in deep debt and had hocked all his family heirlooms. Soon he started selling drugs to pay his creditors. His fits of violence against his new wife were unbearable, sending Lisa to Al-Anon to understand his alcoholic childhood.

As a Catholic, divorce was not an option for her. John wouldn't see an anger counselor, but he kept stalling. Afraid to confide in her family, she was in the darkest, loneliest place she'd ever been.

"I started to pray in earnest and ask God's direction," she says, "though I was still confused." At a WEAVE meeting (Women Escaping A Violent Environment), she listened to horror stories of broken bones, broken hearts, and broken marriages. "Most of these men never get help," said the experts. What a disappointing eye-opener!

Finally she called her mother, who assured her she was doing the right thing to leave the marriage. She felt like a failure. "My biggest regret was not having a child. I couldn't bring a child into a bad marriage, so I resolved not to have children and never be pressured to remarry."

Stripped of her self-esteem, she turned her focus to work in a busy assembly member's office at the California State Capitol. That's where I wander into her story. Lisa was at the front desk when I arrived for my job interview on the fourth floor of the impressively restored building. Because my senator had gone on to Congress, I was seeking a new position in which I could use my state legislative background.

Another appointment for me from God.

Lisa, who looked like a fashion model with satiny gold hair and flawless clothes, was constantly dating. When she asked about *my* social life, I would relate the activities of our Saturday night singles' fellowship. Why didn't I have a boyfriend, she probed. No dates, just men friends? *No sex?* That's odd.

In a casual way I brought up my decision to give those desires to the Lord and to wait on Him for the right man, adding that I'd botched things up pretty badly on my own.

She'd smile and nod and mentally scratch her head. If we had been movie stars, I'd be the relic from the silent screen, religious and very out-of-date. The entire staff dubbed me the "moral compass" of the office.

> *Time is a dressmaker specializing in alternations.*
> —Faith Baldwin

Lisa didn't know it then, but I made certain she had a regular slot on our Friday morning prayer list.

As time rolled on, Lisa drifted in and out of several unsuccessful relationships and became more toughened, more disillusioned. Meanwhile, my emotional roller coaster finally began to level off. I was content in my single life, despite the difficulties with my youngest daughter, Amy, that kept me in counseling once a week. I would come into the office each week offering new insights about setting more boundaries and discovering why my painful past had masked the real Jan, the one God meant me to be.

Lisa had an itch to know more, and I was happy to satisfy her curiosity. She was full of regrets, honest doubt, and a very flimsy faith, but I sensed that God was ready to take it and run the distance in order to show her how much more there is to a life with Him.

I grew bolder every day in sharing how the Lord worked in me.

Then more trials came my way. After several resident counseling programs, Amy appeared to be straightening out and finding peace with herself. She seemed eager to finish her education. But at seventeen she met the wrong guy and became pregnant.

After much soul-searching and examining the reality of raising a baby when she was so confused about life, she decided, "I'm going to put the baby up for adoption." I was proud of her maturity and the way she wanted the child to have a committed father, something she had missed. But I had no idea the swell of emotions that would consume me over the next months as we chose the parents for her baby-girl-to-be.

When that newborn went out our door with her adoptive parents and grandmother, I fell to pieces. My sadness would not lift. As Amy healed, I struggled with yet another loss.

"You were an inspiration to me during that time," Lisa told me recently during our catch-up-on-life lunch. "I'd seen you walk through some amazingly tough times, including the death of both your parents in one year, your daughters' difficulties, and, especially, Amy's pregnancy and giving up her child. Each day seemed to bring a new tragedy back then, but through it all you continued to rely on God. I would just shake my head and wonder how much one person could take. The prevailing peace you had was something I always coveted. When I would dream about what I wanted in life, it was that peace I had seen in people like you who put their trust in God."

The moral compass of the office had become a small beam of light. You never know when God will use your struggles as a signpost for someone else.

To help them find the way to a deeper faith.

Lisa mustered up the courage to try a good counselor and confront her past pain. "What a revelation! I began to see how unhealthy my relationships had been and why I fought so hard for control to keep from facing the pain of the past. After the tears and anger, I finally took ownership of being a victim and faced responsibility for all my wrong choices. Finally I was on the road to being free."

Our Friday morning prayers were paying off in a big way.

Don't ever think God isn't working behind the scenes in government. Every Wednesday at noon in a quiet committee room in the California State Capitol, a group comes together to study and pray. Guess who walked in one day? "I got to know myself all over again during those lunch hours," Lisa says. "And I began to know the real God, not the God of my religious childhood."

After eight years of working together, Lisa and I grew to be dear friends and soul sisters. She began to look to the Lord for answers instead of people. For the first time in her life, she was comfortable with just being Lisa.

Wouldn't you know, that's when the lovebug decided to bite? Friends introduced her to Greg, a much younger man. Not attracted to him at all, Lisa felt quite safe. For a year they were pals, trotting off to the movies, picnics, and boating. "Strange—I had never dated just a friend."

"It was so different from the intense relationships I've had," she says. "His down-to-earth attitude, innocence, and sincerity was refreshing. But what about the eight-year difference in their ages?

"I was thirty-seven. What if I could never have children?" They took solace in the fact that Lisa's mother had had her last child at age forty-five. "The light of hope began to flicker for me to have a baby. Did I dare rekindle that hope?"

Over lunch hours and mocha breaks, we had marathon talks about trusting God through it all, and the couple prayerfully set a wedding date. What a joyous wedding that glorified God! A happy ending at last?

Not quite.

By the time they decided to try for a baby, Lisa was 39. "My doctor reassured me I had the body of a 30-year-old and would have no problem conceiving."

Trouble is often the lever in God's hand to raise us up to heaven.

One small detail. First, she had to have a fibroid tumor removed from her uterus. The weekend before surgery, the Bible study group went on a retreat, prayed, and laid loving hands on Lisa, asking for a baby to come to her soon.

The surgery was no problem. "I was sure it was a sign from God that I was going to have a baby."

Months later, still no conception. Eventually a test revealed she was not releasing any eggs, and it would be impossible to get pregnant. She left in tears from the office after she informed us. When she called Greg, he could barely talk. They cried all weekend together, trying to put their dreams to rest. Greg stood by the window and watched children romp in the playground across the street from their house, tears rolling down his cheeks. "He didn't blame me, but I felt so awful for him. Again I had to come to terms with never having a child."

And the thought crossed her mind, is this a punishment from God for her past mistakes?

She needed a wise word from her mom. "Lisa," she said to her daughter, "put yourself in God's hands. That's all you can do." Immediately, Lisa dried her tears and felt tremendous peace.

Now what? An egg donor was out of the question, once they learned that fertilized eggs are destroyed in the process. Their minister suggested adoption, but Lisa had worked on several adoption bills at the Capitol and had seen the awful possibilities that could happen trying to make someone else's baby your own with California's tangle of adoption laws.

And Greg only wanted "their" child. It looked like they would remain childless, after all. They were learning an important lesson in faith—we must trust God's purposes without knowing why.

In the midst of Lisa's sadness, I offered constant updates about Connie's quest for a foreign adoption, all the red tape, the long wait, and finally the incredible story about Sadie's arrival.

Lisa went from resisting the suggestion of the "a" word to curiosity and interest. When she delicately broached the idea of adopting a foreign child to Greg, he was not open, period! "I understood how he felt since I had been in the same place just a few weeks before. He didn't want just a child, he wanted *our* child," she said.

No more discussion. So we prayed continuously that God would soften Greg's heart. If not, could she accept it and allow God to redirect her dream?

It's always the question we're faced with, isn't it? Do I trust God enough to die to my dreams?

The growth in my friend amazed me. She glowed with the peace of Christ. Her future was in His hands and His time. "I feel like I'm on an adventure, excited to see how God will work in our lives," she said.

A year went by. It was Christmas Eve, and as they were walking in the solitude of Greg's parents' ranch near San Francisco, her husband got choked up. "We do need to bring a child here."

What a Christmas present! He agreed to apply for an adoption.

They immediately registered with a private facilitator. Four months later they received a telephone call from a young college couple in Indiana who felt they were not ready to become parents. They had seen Lisa and Greg's profile on the Internet and were instantly drawn to them.

At forty-three Lisa finally become a mom. Two years ago they brought their newborn daughter home to the house with the park across the street. Because she had turned her ruined dreams over to Him, God had real answers for her real faith. Her dream came true in a slightly different way than she had planned, but it was tailor-made for her.

Lisa responded to her disappointment by calling on God, and He promised her "new wine and oil" (Joel 2:19), a sweet wine, enough to satisfy her fully.

I wish you could see her now.

CHAPTER ELEVEN

A CLEAN SWEEP

Never again will I make you an object of scorn to the nations.
—Joel 2:19

ONE OF THE GALS who came through our singles group works for a large insurance company as an adjuster. When disaster strikes, such as an earthquake or hurricane, she inspects and assesses the damage.

Millie is always a welcome sight to the victims. She's their comforter, their hope of starting the process of rebuilding what has been lost.

For them nothing will be the same again. Many sacred treasures are lost forever: family heirlooms and prized possessions, evidences of hard work and years of dreams. When Millie walks the rubble-strewn lot with the family to survey the damage, they recall in vivid detail how the house looked. They describe each room in detail, down to the pictures hanging on the walls and the new sofa only a week old. She listens as they say goodbye to what was and make plans for what will be.

She will be their link to a restored future.

As we walk with the Lord through our rubble and survey what appears to be a monumental task, we are bonded to Him. His presence becomes real, and there is cause to face another day with the assurance that God alone knows what will become of the empty lot.

Even if we don't have a clue.

Some of the insured clients of Millie's company are both disoriented and perplexed. They can't adjust to the loss, and nothing Millie can say will comfort them until they work through the anger, the bitterness, the "Why me, God?" syndrome. They're now homeless and displaced, facing months and maybe years of uncertainty and change. Who enjoys surveying the ruins of what used to be?

Gerald Sittser, author and religion professor, came to speak at our church last year about loss and its sense of sheer randomness. He knows loss well; a tragic accident, a careless act by a stranger, claimed his mother, his wife, and young daughter. In his book *A Grace Disguised*, he says it is better to brace ourselves for accidents because they are part of life. When disaster comes, it is better not to focus on what is lost but on what is left. It helps avoid the bitterness.[1]

We all agree that forgiveness is a beautiful idea until
we have to practice it.
—C. S. Lewis

One day Ginger's lip quivered as she asked me, "How do I forgive this man? I'm not as angry anymore, and I've lost the urge to strike back, but I just can't forgive him for what he did to me, to all of us."

Again, there are no smart solutions or glib answers for this question. "Forgiveness is a process," I replied with confidence. "It'll come as you press into God."

Nothing I could say would help her shed the resentment. Each journey takes different roads. She and God had to work it out.

I think back on my own treadmill of forgiveness. During my marriage I learned to forgive Bob continuously; I could never hold a grudge when he came to me remorseful over each indiscretion and asked for another chance, yet I guarded my heart each time, slowly inching back into trust. Just when I would relax in my love for my husband, another crisis bowled me over.

When he finally left us, and I ended up at a counselor's office, she confronted me, commenting, "You are full of rage."

Who, me? Not me, I protested in complete denial. But with some candid coaxing, she helped me to recognize my anger and then to spew out the bitter wormwood in my heart.

Still I resolved to remain strong. The battles that loomed ahead—support, property settlement—could not be won in weakness. The man I loved had always wounded me in my weakness.

Never again.

Working through Proverbs one day I read, "If your enemy is hungry, give him food to eat; And if he is thirsty, give him water to drink; for you will heap burning coals on his head. And the LORD will reward you" (Prov. 25:21–22 NASB).

Kindness shown to an enemy will shame him—is that a fact? What an intriguing picture: Bob, with his eyes aglow, his hair steaming and blistering, humming to himself, "What kind of fool am I?"

So this is what Solomon, the wisest of all, advised concerning relationships? Perhaps I would give it a try. When Bob's lawyer presented me with a three-page list of desired household items my mate wished to have—stereo, pewter set, half the kitchen, the antique dresser I refinished—I answered calmly, "He can have it all. Anything he wants."

It felt good not to resist, actually refreshing. My cease-fire brought a sweet peace. I liked this newly gained principle. Suddenly none of these material things were important to me; they wouldn't bring back my shattered hopes and ruined dreams.

And what do you know? Bob lost interest in his inventory list and decided to take only the tools left in the garage.

My first example of God's "open palm plan." For the right actions and attitudes, there is reward.

Still there were more scraps ahead with Bob and his lawyer. Each time I appeared in court, I had to endure my replacement's penetrating eyes; yet I held my head up and my shoulders back, determined not to let them see how much it hurt that he brought *her* to the funeral of our marriage. Afterward, as I let out my sobs in the quiet of my bedroom, my anger bubbled. I hated him again.

Where can we put our hate while we say our prayers?

Oh, yes, I wanted to bury the hatchet—right in the middle of his back.

Jesus said, "For if you forgive people their wrongdoing, your heavenly Father will forgive you as well. But if you don't forgive people, your Father will not forgive your wrongdoing" (Matt. 6:14).

Yeah, but—isn't that what my daughters always said when they scoffed at my nuggets of advice? *Yeah, but he keeps hurting me, Lord. When will justice prevail? How many times do I have to go through this forgiveness thing?*

Peter asked the same thing of Jesus. "As many as seven times?" he inquired, and Jesus answered, "I tell you, not as many as seven, but seventy times seven" (Matt. 8:21–22).

Either way, that's wiping a lot of slates clean. We're talking a whole lot of burials of bygones here.

Unforgiveness is like a fire that smolders in the belly, says Gerald Sittser. It's like smoke that smothers the soul. Unforgiveness, he reminds us, should not be confused with healthy responses to loss. Anger is a legitimate emotional response to suffering. When someone has done something hurtful to us, we want to strike back and hurt them. It's natural.

Unforgiveness comes when bitterness incubates in the soul. It doesn't stop the pain; it spreads it, in rampant force like a winter flu bug. I had enough bugs hovering in my life; I could do without another one.

Sittser also says that forgiveness may not have an ending, but it has a beginning. "It begins when victims identify the wrong done to them and feel the anger that naturally rises in the soul. They realize that what happened to them was inexcusable and should not have happened. Before victims can show mercy, they must claim justice. Before they can forgive, they must accuse."[2]

That's good news. It means we can get hot under the collar and gnash our teeth, spit out all the black bile (even to an empty chair), and *then* we can give up the right to wield a bloody nose and a black eye. We can be merciful, as God is merciful with us. Sinful people need God's forgiveness.

When the property issues were finally settled, when Bob and my replacement moved out of the area (Praise the Lord, no more avoiding them in town), it was much easier to wish them well. It felt noble to pray for them, that they would discover God's incredible love.

But each time one of the girls struggled with an absent-father issue, I'd feel the bitterness well up again like an oil gusher. He had squashed my dreams—that I could tolerate—but hurting my babies was inexcusable.

Again, I had to forgive, get on my knees and give it over. If I believed that God could make beauty out of my ashes, I had to trust He could do it with my daughters, even if I couldn't see evidence of it yet. While their earthly father shunned them for his new family, their heavenly Father waited to embrace and heal them.

Wait and trust. It was out of my hands.

Eventually both my girls yielded to Christ. Amy found Him through the struggles in her hasty marriage to Jesse, and Jennifer did after exhausting every other avenue to fulfillment. Yet Jen still struggled with her *"Daddy, where were you?"* questions. Several years after she married Steve, Jen's distrust and anger at men oozed out slowly, and her quest for control began to unravel their relationship. Steve was at his wit's end, asking advice on how to handle her. I stepped in to try and talk sense into Jenny, but she always cut me off.

Until she cut me off completely.

Then one morning in 1998, after partying with a girlfriend at a local club, Jen was driving up the rainy mountain highway at high speed without her seat belt. Her car hit the center divide and flipped upside down, along with my world as I knew it.

At the trauma center the doctor reported, "She's not dead, but she's in pretty bad shape. She's in a coma with a severe head injury."

Sometimes a single moment can change everything.

When I first saw my daughter with the right side of her face swollen and her flesh discolored in shades of maroon, with clear plastic tubing in her nostrils and beeping monitors in her half-shaved head, I flinched. Was this a dream? My fiesty little girl helpless in a coma? Thrown a hundred feet from the sunroof? Will she die with a wall between us? I'd prayed for God to intervene, to stop her self-destruction, but this?

Will these nightmares never end?

Some amount of brain damage was expected, maybe paralysis, so many possibilities we didn't know yet.

God surely did, and I had no choice but to summon all the evidence of His trustworthiness, all my faith in His perfect plan.

Are you testing my faith, Lord? Surely, you have a purpose for this. I'll trust you even though I don't understand.

Five days later, as I stood and leaned over her bed rail praying for the pressure to decrease in her brain, I heard the last few words of an ICU nurse's announcement, ". . . is here to see his daughter."

He's here? After seven years?

"I'll handle this," I piped, biting my lip, steadying myself. I checked my weary face, fluffed my hair, and met my ex-husband in the hallway. After seven years of total silence, Bob had reappeared with that conscience-stricken look on his face I recognized so well.

He took one look at his daughter with her half-shaved head. "Can we talk somewhere, please?" he asked.

My defenses told me not to indulge him, but here was the man who had been the husband of my youth. Surely he had shared the same "forever" dreams as I had in our early marriage and had come into our union with a belief that it would last. Who would ever say their marriage vows with a hint of leaving someday?

I had to remind myself: *Jan, it was Bob's exit from your life that sent you into the arms of your Lord.*

So, in the quiet of an overflow visitor's room, my former husband hung his head and began to speak. "It's all my fault. She's just like me. Reckless, running away from her pain. If I hadn't left you, this would never have happened. I'm so sorry I messed up our marriage."

I could never have scripted a scene like this, though my fantasies had heard those words many times. What a tongue-lashing I could give the man now, with a velvet glove, of course. I could dole out every reason why he should regret what he did to us. I could let him hear how much he had hurt me. After all, he deserved it, didn't he?

Ready to deliver a monologue, my jaws opened, but nothing spilled out except God's grace. "I forgive you, Bob."

And then I asked him to forgive me for pressuring him against returning to Vietnam years ago. In my ignorance and love, I had kept him from his duty and his self-respect. With uncontrolled sobs he fell into my arms, and we wept together.

For forty-five minutes we talked about yesterday, today, and the future. He promised to be a part of our girls' lives again and to make up for the pain of not being around in their teen years. I wanted so much to believe him for our daughters' sake.

Was it too much to hope for? I'd believed him so many times before.

The very next day Jenny emerged from her coma, to the doctor's amazement. "Unbelievable," he said. "This girl is going to recover." After three months in a rehabilitation hospital, after learning to walk, talk, eat, and put on makeup again, Jenny came home with a hopeful prognosis from the doctors that she would be nearly as good as before.

What do they know? I laughed inwardly. Unbelievable to the experts maybe, but not to me. God isn't finished with this girl yet; she will be *better* than before.

"I never want to be estranged from you again, Mom," she said with a crooked smile. "I see now how very much you love me, and I want to grow close to the Lord."

Bob's promises didn't last long. As soon as Jenny seemed well on her way to recovery, he reverted back to the old ways. His calls are short, infrequent, and shallow. Never a Christmas present or a birthday card.

A few weeks ago he disappointed her again, and I finally popped. Let's not describe what kind of snarling came out of me. For a few hours I fumed, gnashed my teeth, and threw mental daggers at him, the man who had hurt my babies, had abandoned them as children, and had left our life in shambles. The man who doesn't even let his daughters have his home telephone number, only the one at the office. (*She* doesn't want the girls to call their home.)

My eyes do a furious dance just thinking about it.

Though I know better than to take up Jenny's offense, this rage engulfed me because Bob can still, after all these years, inflict so much pain. Over the phone with Amy, I spewed out my feelings. "He doesn't deserve either one of you! It would be better if he didn't exist. He'll only keep hurting you both. Why do you have to have anything to do with him at all?"

She paused and softly said, "I realize I can't depend on him or believe anything he says, Mom, but God wants me to honor him as my father."

Gulp. Good thing she couldn't see my lowered eyes and red face. Just when I think I'm on a spiritual high plain, that I'm above and beyond bitter bones about him, there they stand stacked in front of me ten feet high. Reminders that my for-giveness clock is ticking backwards.

A relapse into resentment.

"Mom, I used to hate him for destroying my life, for all the drugs I took to numb the pain, for the men I got involved with looking to be loved, for a pregnancy I wasn't ready for and the daughter I gave up. But the hate was eating me alive. Just recently, after another broken promise he'd made, I spent days praying and sobbing to the Lord to release *me*. And nothing. Finally I understood that *I* had to release *him*, or I would never be free."

Then she added, "Someday Dad will ask me questions about the Lord, and I want to show him Christ living in me. Maybe it will make a difference. I have to hope it will."

My lip grew stiff; tears swelled. How many times had I encouraged my daughters to see things from a heavenly per-spective? "'For my thoughts are not your thoughts, neither are your ways my ways,' declares the Lord. 'As the heavens are higher than the earth, so are my ways higher than your ways'" (Isa. 55:8).

Faith had changed Amy's attitude about the man who'd wounded her so many times, who'd left her wondering if she was worth loving. Faith had given her a "God's eye view."

She saw the situation from a divine perch, while her mother screeched about the man from a crow's nest. One view from a heavenly window, the other only from a peephole.

Weren't these the very precepts I had taught these girls? How casually they can slip away unawares in the heat of the moment!

"Mom, have you ever wondered what would have hap-pened if Dad had never left you, and if we'd have lived in Greenwood without all the trouble that came?"

I knew exactly where she was going with this one. "Yes, of course."

"I doubt you'd be the woman you are today. You poured into us all that God taught you through what you endured.

And if it weren't for you sending me to Christian Encounter Ranch and all those other teen programs, if it weren't for you constantly trying to get me on the right path, being the godly example you are, I'd never love the Lord today."

Speechless in Auburn—that was me. I tried to clear what felt like a burr in my throat. Beauty from ashes. That's what He always makes if we ask and believe, I remember thinking.

Forgive me, Lord. I felt the tension leave my neck and shoulders. I could clearly hear the sweet sound of God's melody of mending.

> *Forgiveness is a funny thing—*
> *it warms the heart and cools the sting.*
> —Agnes Sanford

I'd been clipping along with this book in record time to get it to the publisher. Yet, when I came to this chapter where I planned to mention the forgiveness process, I began to fritter away the time, dawdling to avoid sitting down at the computer. Taking a walk, digging in the garden, searching for inspiration. Then this call from Amy, and God showed me that I needed, once again, to forgive Bob.

How many times again, Lord? I'm reminded that, in Hebrew, "seventy times seven" refers to infinity. We go on forgiving *forever* those who have wronged us. It doesn't mean we entirely forget, nor does it mean we remember with bitterness.

Maybe Bob needs to sweep occasionally through my life so I can get more practice in granting a pardon. I can only imagine how my former mate tries to suppress his own pain and guilt at what he's done and hasn't done. Or how he handles the burning coals on his head.

One thing for sure, it's not up to me, nor will it ever be, to pass sentence. Amy is right. God still loves her father and still wants to come into his life.

Someday I'd like to tell Bob how God has used him to scrub me up, to help me shed the grit, to teach me the discipline of brushing off the bitterness. To make the clean sweep. Someone once said, as we grow in wisdom, we pardon more freely.

My friend Cindy is a wise woman who learned to forgive the most horrible thing imaginable, a malicious act against her child. In 1995 she got a telephone call that her daughter Heidi had been burned and was being sent from Arkansas to a burn unit in Missouri. The nurse said, "If you want to see your daughter alive again, you'd better get on a plane right away." When she and her husband Rudy arrived, they were told that Heidi would probably not last the night.

"I was not prepared to see what I saw lying there," Cindy told me. "I did not recognize my daughter." Her entire body was bandaged, except her feet, three little fingers and her head. She clutched the curtain around the bed wondering if she would be able to stand up.

"I ran from the room crying out to God in desperation," she said. "Anger came over me as I raced back in to my daughter's bedside, crying and telling her I was going to find out who did this!"

But in her heart she knew.

Heidi had been running from God for ten years. Divorced and with two toddlers, she moved to Arkansas with a man who sold drugs and supplied her with all she wanted. Because she'd been warned that her grandchildren were in danger, Cindy and Rudy flew to Arkansas and pressed for temporary custody until Heidi could straighten out her life.

She was trying to do just that. With her bags packed in the car, Heidi told Bobby she was leaving him for good, but he had different plans. He threw gasoline over the car, set it on fire, and left her in a field to die.

Miraculously, a friend happened to find her.

"I kept reminding myself, as I walked up and down the halls, that I was not alone. God was in this with us," she said. "I could have collapsed if my faith was not strong."

That Sunday, after being at the hospital for several days, the exhausted couple mustered up enough strength to walk to a nearby church. Through the sermon, Cindy felt the Lord whisper comforting words. "And I told God that, no matter what happened, my prayer was that people would be drawn to Him through Heidi's tragic experience," she told me.

Even Bobby? The Lord seemed to say. "Even Bobby," she promised.

Back at Heidi's bedside, Cindy asked her dying daughter, "Honey, have you accepted Jesus as your Lord and Savior?" Heidi nodded yes.

"I saw a peace in her, and then peace flooded my heart. My daughter would not die without the Lord. She was going to heaven." Cindy started singing songs to her. Rudy read her Bible verses, and they prayed continually.

Before the police arrested Bobby, he came to the hospital. At first Cindy cried to the nurse, "Get him. He's the one!" But when she walked to the waiting room and saw Bobby with his head in his hands, she felt a calming assurance. "I knew that if I had bitterness, hatred, and an unforgiving spirit, my prayers would go unheard. I knew I had to forgive Bobby, and with the Lord's help I did. I knew that Jesus could forgive Bobby too, because there is never a sin too big that the blood of Jesus can't cover." She told him, "Jesus loves you, Bobby. I pray that through all this you get your life together."

Local churches found out about Heidi, and Cindy was asked if she would share the story. "I knew God was in control of my daughter's spiritual and physical needs—in control over every breath she took. I knew she was all squared away with Him. Now it was time to turn it around and let God use it for good." In the midst of the ordeal, she spoke at three churches to share the love of God.

"People began to respond," she said. "I had a tremendous opportunity to share about Jesus, especially at the hospital with the nurses and doctors. Only with the supernatural help of the Holy Spirit could I be running around speaking at that time. Only through the Lord could I truly forgive Bobby."

After twenty-one days Heidi finally died. "And she wasn't expected to last forty-eight hours," Cindy exclaims. "She could have died in that field where she was left, but she was given twenty-one days to make things right with her Heavenly Father. What a blessing! And if the children hadn't been with us, they would have burned too."

"Today life is full, better than ever," she says. She speaks to Christian women's clubs, to youth groups, even to young lpeople in prisons about our consequences, about forgiveness, about death and making sure we know where we're going after we die.

She and Rudy are Mommy and Daddy now to Heidi's children, ages eight and ten. "My husband lives with regrets that, as Heidi's stepfather, he didn't do enough when she was young. Now he has been given a chance to make up. And now that we're older and much wiser, there is so much joy in parenting. God has truly restored my years in so many ways."

I don't know about you, but if Cindy can forgive the man who murdered her daughter, I can forgive those who've wounded me.

Are you straining to forgive someone right now? Someone who has wounded you? Remember what Joel said after the priests cried, "Spare your people, O Lord" (Joel 2:17). God extended His mercy, with these reassuring words, "Never again will I make you an object of scorn to the nations" (Joel 2:19).

He was referring to the locust plague, but we can bank on this promise: If we accept the invitation to forgive and be forgiven, He'll keep us far from disgrace and humiliation.

You may never hear a cry for clemency or a request for forgiveness from someone who hurt you, but take a crack at it anyway. Like me, you may have to wipe the slate clean over and over and over again, but that's OK. It's a great workout.

Think of it this way; you're building your mercy muscle.

CHAPTER TWELVE

GREAT EXPECTATIONS—SEE THE WIND BLOW

I will drive the northern army far from you,
pushing it into a parched and barren land.
—Joel 2:20

DRUM ROLL. BUGLE CALL. The bugs are taking flight. This verse from chapter 2 is certainly the turning point in the book of Joel. Although we don't get specifics, we can assume that the people did respond to the prophet's plea to return their hearts to God, so the Lord promises to scatter the ravaging bugs to the desert.

Brighter days are on the way.

I wonder if some of the farmers and townspeople still wrestled with disbelief, still suffered from shell shock when they heard Joel say, "Surely he has done great things. Be not afraid, O land; be glad and rejoice. Surely the Lord has done great things" (Joel 2:21).

"Do not be afraid?" they may have uttered. "I've lived in fear and hunger for so long I'm used to it. Great things? Show me what they are, if you may, Lord. Then I'll rejoice, OK?"

Joel then called everybody who suffered, even the wild animals, to cast off their fears and celebrate. "The open pastures are becoming green. The trees are bearing their fruit; the fig tree and the vine yield their riches" (Joel 2:22).

This prophet is so certain of what is to come that he speaks as if it has already happened! Now that's optimism. And God used the activities of a horde of lowly insects as His object lesson.

A friend of mine, Eva Marie, once received another heavenly lesson from the locust's cousin, a grasshopper. The critter basked on her window ledge once in the warm sunshine, she told me, "his wings periodically quivering in the gentle breeze." She noticed that one of his back legs was missing, and his antennae worked furiously, guiding him. "Inch by inch, push by push, with only five legs and the wind force against him, he finally reached his goal and fluttered away."

The bug's toil served as a good example for Eva Marie when her wings were clipped by disaster. Years ago she and her husband had the world by the tail, anxious to share their monetary harvest with the less fortunate. Then along came a business opportunity that looked so appealing that it must be a gift from God. Eight months later, to their horror, they found it was merely the devil's ploy. They had put their faith in a farce. Soon they had drained their savings, sold their possessions, and filed for bankruptcy. Finally came the shame of government assistance, welfare, and food stamps.

They'd gone from graceful givers to resistant receivers. "It's uncomfortably humbling," she says. "First, I had to work through the anger at the person behind the farce. Then there were those days when I walked to the mailbox, asking God how we would pay the rent or the electric bill. I'd nearly collapse to my knees to find an unexpected check, given to help us meet our needs." She would often stand before the empty refrigerator praying about what to do for dinner. Often, before she shut the door, the phone would ring, and she would hear, "Hi there. Just wanted to know if you were free for dinner tonight. We're buying."

Time and time again it happened. Yet with all the miracles that took place, one tops them all—the miracle in her heart.

"Never had I clung to the Word of God as I did during that trial. Never had I felt His comforting hand on my shoulder, His wisdom growing inside me, His hope pressing me on."

Wounded and battered like the grasshopper on her window, Eva Marie turned her face to the wind of optimism. "I kept seeing the prize, the promises of God for His faithful," she says. "They would be there. I envisioned them, and I never gave up believing they would come in time."

And they did. In 1999, her husband's business soared, they were able to buy their own home, and her first book was published. The couple formed their own ministry, SARAH (Sharing and Restoring Adds Hope).

Recently, when they heard of a young woman who needed a bed, they walked into the mattress store to buy her one. They are again the givers God designed them to be. Eva Marie says, "I learned that God has a great deal for me to do and that what I have to offer has little to do with earthly wealth. It was an awesome discovery that I would never have made without enduring the storm in my life. Now here I am in ministry, helping people in need in the same position I experienced myself. How much better I am for it, how much more I understand about the character of my Lord—because I lost everything."

In the bleakest of times, Eva Marie waited in optimistic anticipation for what God would do when the storm was over. "It helped the fog of futility to evaporate," she says. With new clarity she entered into a new intimacy with God.

Let's not forget what Habakkuk tells us about waiting for the vision that seems to be delayed.

When you're in limbo, don't circle the runway confused in the fog because you can't see the field. Envision that perfect three-point landing now. OK, so you're caught in zero visibility with low fuel. Take heart, for God is up in the air-traffic control tower in complete charge of this mission. In due time He'll flip on those fog lights.

We all hope for the best, but an optimist expects it.

I have a gnarled old apricot tree in my backyard. As I write this it is winter, and it looks grim and sterile, but if this tree is true to character, it will burst with buds in the spring. It will yield fruit that will drop all over the ground and invite the ants. When the apricots decide to ripen (all at once) I am seldom enthusiastic about canning or making jam. It's never the right timing. Della, from prayer breakfast, is overjoyed at my lack of kitchen zeal. She has laid a claim to first pickings this summer. Even now she waits with optimistic anticipation for late June, when she will haul over her ladder and go to work.

And she's counting on a bumper crop this year.

Hebrews 11:13 says that the great heroes of the faith died "without having received the promises, but they saw them from a distance" and "greeted them."

Faith lays hold of promises from far off. When God told Abraham, "Leave your country, your people and your father's household and go to the land I will show you" (Gen. 12:1), he obeyed, confident that the blessing of the Lord would make up for all he could ever lose or leave behind.

That's faith. He didn't know the way, but he knew the guide.

Did he have questions? Most certainly, but he was also certain they would all be answered in time. God's plan would exceed all the desires he would ever have. That's sky-high optimism, refusing to let the difficulties and delays be too discouraging, being ready to persevere to the end.

> Keep your face to the sunshine
> and you cannot see the shadow.
> —Helen Keller

When my daughter Amy was in her prodigal years, fourteen to seventeen, I waited nervously for the ax to fall, for the dreaded phone call from a hospital emergency room to tell me she'd been hurt. By this time I felt relief when the calls merely came from the jail. At least she was safe. Amy paraded around with a gang that experimented in everything from dope to devil worship. I'd wake up at night with dreadful thoughts that wouldn't go away.

One morning Mary Gail called and told me to read Acts 2. "I've been praying for Amy this morning, and during my devotions I came across this verse. It's a promise from God for our children!" My dear friend is a great example of a diligent and praying mother.

I turned to the passage, and I read about the preaching on that day of Pentecost when Peter declared that it was Jesus who sent the Holy Spirit.

"When they heard this, they were pierced to the heart." They asked what they should do. "'Repent,' Peter said, 'and tbe baptized . . . and you will receive the gift of the Holy Spirit'" (Acts 2:37–38).

I had read Acts before, but when I saw verse 39, "The promise is for you and your children, and for all who are far off, as many as the Lord our God will call," the words vaulted off the page!

Far off. So far off. Sometimes I never heard from my daughter for months and wondered if she was even alive, but here in this verse the Lord was telling me that if I were a true believer, He would call my daughter home.

The delivery date might still remain a mystery, but the postage was guaranteed.

From that day on I pledged to see both my daughters through God's eyes, not mine. In my limited vision I could only see the awful things that happen in dark places and dangerous streets, but God would turn the gnarls and knots and strings of their rebellion into a beautiful tapestry.

He had a blueprint in the works for their lives—one very different from mine. He knew what they would ultimately become, no matter how it seemed to my limited sight.

Jesus changed the disciple Simon's name to *Peter*, which meant "rock." When Peter first walked with Christ, he was anything but a symbol of stability. Impulsive and slow to understand the mysteries of faith, Peter often had his foot in his mouth. He even assured his Master he would never disown Him, but Jesus said, "Tonight—before the rooster crows, you will deny Me three times!"

"I will never deny you!" cried Peter (Matt. 26:34–35). Perish the thought! But Jesus knew him better than he knew himself.

"Simon, Simon, Satan has asked to sift you like wheat. But I have prayed for you, that your faith may not fail. And you, when you have turned back, strengthen your brothers" (Luke 22:31).

Peter's test would be severe, full of guilt, shame, and doubt, but when we see him again in Acts, Peter is firm and courageous, a preacher and interpreter of the Scripture. What a convincing proof of the power of Christ! As promised, Peter would fortify the faith of the other disciples as they spread the Gospel to the world.

If you've never read the classic *Hinds' Feet on High Places* by Hannah Hurnard, please put it on your to-buy list. It's a charming allegory of yearning to reach new heights. It's the story of Much-Afraid, a cripple, who lives in the Valley of Humiliation in the village of Much-Trembling. When the Shepherd invites her to go to the High Places, she fears the mountains are too steep and dangerous for one so lame.

"It is quite true that the way up to the High Places is both difficult and dangerous," says the Shepherd. "It has to be, so that nothing which is an enemy of Love can make the ascent and invade the Kingdom."

He promises Much-Afraid that He will make her feet like hinds' (mountain goats') feet and set her upon high places. There she can serve Him and be out of the way of her enemies.

Her journey is hard, and her two companions are Sorrow and Suffering, but slowly she overcomes her tormenting fears. She passes through many dangers with the Shepherd as her guide and finally comes to the healing streams. "At last," the Shepherd says, "at last you are here and the night of weeping is over and joy comes to you in the morning." Then, lifting her up, he continues, "This is the time when you are to receive the fulfillment of the promise. Never am I to call you Much-Afraid again."

He changes her name to Grace and Glory.

With her new name she returns to her valley, transformed, ready to help those who still live in misery and loneliness.

God's in His heaven. All's right with the world.
—Robert Browning

I stopped referring to Jenny as my "rebel" and Amy as "my prodigal, my lost one" but as "my lovely child of God."

My thoughts changed to ones of optimistic anticipation: Jenny will soften. Amy will come back home. Their bruised hearts will heal; they'll be better than before.

I never had another sleepless night over my daughters, although it took seven years for Amy to turn around, to merge into God's plan for her life. Yes, she's suffered some consequences for her foolish choices. But look at her now, with lessons to teach her mother.

Take hold of the words of Jeremiah 29:11: "'For I know the plans I have for you,' declares the Lord, 'plans to prosper you and not to harm you, plans to give you hope and a future.'"

It's helpful to keep in mind the audience Jeremiah is speaking to—people who face captivity in Babylon for seventy more years! He is urging them to await God's deliverance.

I'll bet that this guy didn't get voted Prophet of the Year by anybody. Still the Lord spoke through Jeremiah. "'The days are coming . . . when I will bring my people Israel and Judah back from captivity and restore them to the land I gave their forefathers'" (Jer. 30:3).

God's future blessings would include health, physical and emotional healing, restored fortunes, and honor. He would turn mourning into dancing. In a later chapter He says, "'I have loved you with an everlasting love; I have drawn you with loving-kindness. I will build you up again'" (Jer. 31:3–4). `

The glitch is, He never says how or when. Yet we are to believe with eagerness that He *will* drive the northern armies away. And when they're gone, we can celebrate. He'd probably be thrilled if we start the party before the bugs hit the friendly skies and dash to their doom.

> *Never think that God's delays are God's denials.*
> *Hold on, hold fast, hold out.*
> —Count de Buffon

Before we got into World War II in 1941, England was alone in the battle for world domination by the Nazis. British Prime Minister Winston Churchill told his people, "You ask, what is our aim? I can answer in one word; victory, victory at all costs, victory in spite of the terror, victory, however long and hard the road may be; without victory, there is no survival."

Though Hitler overran almost all of Europe, this little island country wouldn't give up. It was Churchill's invincible spirit, his faith in the cause to fight evil that kept England's people going during those frightening years. His positive outlook girded them up and constantly held victory before them, no matter how many bombs exploded, no matter how bleak things appeared.

Appearances aren't all what they seem.

After we've looked back at the past and done our crying over it, it's helpful to remember what the Lord says. "Do not call to mind the former things, Or ponder things of the past. Behold, I will do something new, Now it will spring forth; Will you not be aware of it?" (Isa. 43:18–19 NASB)

If we glance back too much, we might miss the glory in front of us.

We never get eyestrain from looking on the bright side.

Charles Dickens may have written *Great Expectations*, but he did not originate the idea of expecting the best; our God did. He doesn't want to give us the expectation of our fears, nor the expectation of our whims, but the great expectations of our faith.

CHAPTER THIRTEEN

CLOSING RANKS

Surely he has done great things. Be not afraid.
—Joel 2:21

NADINE'S HUSBAND was our family physician in Greenwood. He treated my girls' broken bones, our flu bugs, and my perpetual poison oak. Bob fixed their family cars, and the doctor fixed our family. Their daughter Christine, the same age as Jenny, signed up for my 4-H sewing class one season. My first and only sewing class, mind you. We attempted several sewing projects, but I soon learned that the only thing a group of chattering nine-year-olds will successfully finish is the exasperated leader.

I wouldn't have missed a minute of it.

Christine had cystic fibrosis, yet this amiable girl seemed unruffled by an illness that kept her in and out of the hospital. At eleven she knew the disease would soon claim her life. "Mommy, I'm scared," she told Nadine the week she died. "Will you read to me from the Bible?"

Nadine had no Bible in the house, but her best friend Annie brought one over, a children's version with vivid pictures. Nadine sat with her dying child on her lap and read from the Old Testament stories familiar from her childhood in Catholic school, the words from the Sermon on the Mount, where Jesus said, "Leave the children alone, and don't try to keep them from coming to Me, because the kingdom of heaven is made up of people like this" (Matt. 19:14).

"Don't be afraid," Nadine assured her daughter, stifling her tears. "You are going where you'll feel no more pain. You're going to be with Jesus."

Her 4-H friends came to say good-bye. Christine willed all her precious things to family and friends, then died quietly at home.

As women often do during crisis time, Nadine performed like a trooper for her family, but after Christine was buried in the little pioneer cemetery in Greenwood, she went into shock and virtually undercover for nearly two years. The doctor couldn't save his own child and took Christine's death hard.

Storm clouds brewed for this couple.

They poured themselves into building a house on ten acres nearby, tending their two younger daughters and some prized Arabian horses. One day I found myself invited to a Bible study at Annie's house.

We prayed for needs of the community and always for Nadine, unceasing prayers for her wounded spirit. "We have to intercede for those too weak and heartbroken," Annie would say.

With bowed heads and clasped hands, these women lifted up Nadine's crushed spirit. I wondered how many prayers had gone up for me in living rooms across town. Prayers from the warriors in God's underground.

Nadine was on every prayer list in the community. Annie shared with her friend how much Christ could do for her in her grief, how she could see Christine again one day.

Yet Nadine couldn't see beyond her grief. Though she knew since Christine's birth that her daughter was on loan for a short time, the finality was overwhelming, the pain inextinguishable. In her deep mourning she shunned company, with the exception of Annie and a neighbor on the adjacent property.

A few years later her husband closed up shop and took a clinic job in Sacramento, ending his private practice. Long hours, a long commute, and he was not home much.

Nadine finally decided to take her daughters to our church. She heard the pastor speak about the Holy Spirit, about making a simple and sincere declaration of faith and being filled with new understanding, new acceptance, new life.

She no longer resisted and felt a stirring in her soul she'd never known before. She came into the faith and out of her den of despair at the same time.

But her husband wanted no part of it. The more she read her Bible and shared the joy that only God's love can bring, the more the doctor's anger drove them apart.

"I don't want Jesus in bed with us," he demanded. "I don't want Him first in your life. You make the choice. It's either me or God."

How could this be? She had finally found comfort in her sorrow and a hope in Christine's death. She appealed to him, "I can love you the way I should love you only because God is first in my life."

But he wouldn't buy it. "The marriage is over. I want you to go."

A new nightmare came, only this time she had no forewarning. Finding God, then losing a marriage? This really happens? She prayed about what she should do. "I had no money, only a part-time job as an aide for the elementary school," she reminded me the other day. "I didn't know if I should fight for the house. I couldn't afford the payments, even with support from him. What should I do, Lord? I asked. And the Lord pressed on my heart this message: You can leave this house. I'll take care of you."

Two weeks before Christmas she and the girls moved into a rental house, living out of an ice chest and sleeping on the floor on inflatable mattresses. Sitting with their Charlie Brown tree in an empty living room, they all cried.

When I heard, I rushed to her house and barely recognized the woman who greeted me at the door. She looked more like a survivor of the German blitz on London than anyone I knew. It was like seeing my own face a few years earlier.

She really wasn't too keen on chatting with me, a reminder of what she faced, a life of singleness, something she'd never imagined. "What will I do?" she asked me. "I've been a home-maker all my life. It's all I know, all I've ever wanted to be."

"Come to our Monday night Bible study. We'll be there for you. We'll pray it through. The answers will come."

So she came, like a zombie, but she came. "I was so depressed for over a year," she explains now. "The group was a lifesaver for me." She started seeing Della, who is a licensed marriage and family therapist. "She helped me through it, too, helped me find direction."

Once in a while we heard Nadine's laugh, which, trans-lated, meant that hope will come again.

My point is this: The restoration process from one sorrow is sometimes intercepted by additional casualties. Remember that God will always send other people to rally around you and to batter the gates of heaven with prayers for you.

Through counseling, Nadine made a firm commitment not to date for two years. Two years to the week, she sat on my deck during a summer party and locked eyes with the only stranger in the crowd, invited at the last minute by someone.

So began a wild, romantic ride and a worry for the rest of us.

I thought of what Ginger Rogers once said in a movie I've long forgotten: "When two people are in love, they don't look at each other; they look in the same direction."

This man had no interest in church or a relationship with God. Déjà vu, a reminder from the past that Nadine yearned to ignore. When she casually mentioned the relationship to Della, our resident counselor never criticized but merely helped her clarify.

"It crushed me to give him up," Nadine admits, "but I had to. It wasn't healthy at all." From January to August she slumped around, weary from it all but determined to be true to God no matter what. In November she called me in a quiet quandary. "Mark asked me out," she said. "My daughter says I should go. What do you think? I'm really not attracted to him at all."

I grinned. *That's good.* We'd known Mark for a while. He was a regular at Saturday night singles group, very witty and extremely nice, and had a track record of commitment to the Lord.

"Go on the date," I said. "Just have a good time."

Boy, did they! Eight months later they were married in my backyard.

> *God is growing in my soul, making it bigger*
> *and filling it with himself.*
> —Gerald Sittser

Eileen had been a widow for thirteen years when we first met. She told me her story.

Her husband, Tom, was diving along the California coast with his best friend and suddenly drowned.

A month after Tom's accident, two young men from their church were heroically rescued after their boat capsized in the very same bay that had taken Tom's life. Questions nagged Eileen: *Why God? Why did you save these two, and not Tom? You could have saved him, too.*

"I felt betrayed," she says. "I wished it was a bad movie that I could rewind, take back, and exchange for another one."

Alone, with a nine-month-old daughter, and pregnant, Eileen wished there was a grief pill you could take to make it go away. "Though I wasn't, I can understand why people are drawn to numbing drugs."

In the years since Tom's death, she's gone through many stages of grief, recovery, and growth. "I remember being mad at the Disney fairy-tale philosophy that society puts on us, the happily ever after. I remember thinking that my life was ruined because even if I could put it back together again with someone else later on, it would never be the original. My children would never have their own father."

A year ago she told me, "I've been trying to trust God beyond logic for years, but I keep remembering the helpless feeling of being there, at God's allowance, and wondering how I could ever trust Him again. He let it happen. Will there be another whammy to disrupt my life and rip my heart out again?"

A year ago she told me she felt like a "three-legged chair with one leg missing, always off-kilter." As I finished writing this book, we touched base. "I'd been trying to nail down God with an airtight guarantee that nothing like it would ever happen again."

God doesn't extend those kind of money-back guarantees— not that I'm aware of.

"I'm beginning to get it," she said, "and it's cool! God has been teaching me this past year that He is my all. He wants to be whatever I need to be a complete woman; my teacher, my best friend, my counselor, my mentor, my father, the unconditional love of my soul."

Her husband had always longed to go east, to visit Washington D.C., to tour the Smithsonian, to stroll through historic Williamsburg, and to see the Civil War battlefields. Recently she and the kids decided to fulfill Dad's dream and made the trek all the way from California. "I was exhilarated that I actually did it, scared along the way, but I did it!"

Carry your own lantern, and you need not fear the dark.
—Jewish Proverb

This past year she's been to seminars and retreats that stretched her faith, and she is developing a "rubber meets the road" practical connection with God.

Eileen is finally discovering her strengths and uniqueness and is having the courage to follow her own dreams. "I'm the evolving woman that belongs to God," she adds. "This summer I'm going on an archaeological dig. I am so excited."

If e-mails could have voices, I would have heard a squeal with that one.

Sometimes it may take a long, long time for your fields to be restored. Don't be in a hurry. Know that someone is praying for you even now, lifting you up to the Lord, praying for protection, strength, and guidance.

Nadine and Eileen were never alone in their struggles. The Lord's army is always nearby. Joel tells the people, "Be not afraid, O land; be glad and rejoice. Surely the LORD has done great things" (Joel 2:21). He stands ready to send out the rear guard to cover for us when we're too weary, weak, and battle scarred.

Isaiah says, "Then your light will break forth like the dawn, and your healing will quickly appear; then your righteousness will go before you, and the glory of the LORD will be your rear guard" (Isa. 58:8).

He will never let you out of His sight.

CHAPTER FOURTEEN

HITCHED TO THE PLOW WITH GOD

For he has given you the autumn rains in righteousness.
—Joel 2:23

HAVE YOU BEEN WONDERING what's been up with Ginger? The last we saw her, she was trying to forgive her former husband. She soon learned the tricks of the trade, that in this game of perpetual forgiveness she would be shuffling the cards for a while. It takes the sting out of some of the bug bites, though, don't you think? Knowing that we can throw those cards down on the table in complete frustration, and each time God will gently hand them back again for the next round.

No questions asked.

Along with the wisdom I often gain from Scarlett O'Hara come nuggets of truth from Oswald Chambers. He reminds us that first we must surrender our whole way of looking at things, and then the Lord will show us what we need to surrender next, and on and on from there.[1] It's like a good old game of "fish." Are you holding the "ace of anger" card? How about the "club of control"?

Hand them over, won't you?

Ginger started to blossom the year after the loss of her marriage. With the divorce final and half the proceeds from the sale of their house in hand, she decided to explore a new start, a change of scenery. "Do you think I should?" she asked me. "I've never liked it here in the foothills, way too hot and dry."

That's for sure. They don't call the Sacramento Valley the "Breadbasket of California" for no reason.

"Where will you look?"

"The Oregon coast, I think. I have an old friend up there."

"Female?"

"Jan! Of course."

Just had to ask. The new bounce in her step made me a bit curious.

"It's wonderful," I said. "And you'll have a friend to encourage you, keep you accountable. See, you have options now."

Secretly, I envied her a bit. Her boys were out on their own, and she had nothing holding her in Auburn. Starting out fresh, pioneering in a new life, what an adventure!

"I know I still have work to do," she said. "And I'm willing. God is right beside me."

"Yep, you're hitched to His plow."

So she wanted to head out for Oregon. . . . I thought of the early pioneers, plodding over the dusty trail from Missouri in wagons loaded with dreams. They were on their way to an unknown place they dubbed Eden's Gate, the land of milk and honey—Oregon. Some were farmers who had fallen on hard times in the East, some left sorrows and mistakes behind, and others were risk takers ready to claim a piece of the American wilderness.

Because of those who had gone before on this same path, each wagon train knew about the obstacles and difficulties ahead. They set out well-stocked, with crates full of tools, bags full of seeds, and bushels of hope.

Ginger had an ample measure of hope now, from those that had been through the wilderness before her. She had pulled herself up off the porch of regret, bought some overalls and a straw hat, and stood ready to venture out in the heat and the clay soil, to meet the Lord and get to work. She had abandoned her quest for immediate answers and closure, stopped asking for the details of what was to come, and the how, when, and where. Instead of demanding new truth, she was ready to act on those truths she already knew.

Before God can make a heart into a garden, he has to first plow it.
—Oswald Chambers

Remember, God never dozes off. God is never napping on His throne up there while we toil through the pain. He is shaken by our grief and concerned with our growth. He is up before daybreak monitoring the events of our life, drawing us closer to Him every day.

Through her prayers and inspirational reading, the Lord soothed Ginger's soul. Through the friendships with other women surviving loss, He gave her hope and the courage to wait it out. And He was waiting, too, for the right time to roll up his sleeves and join her in tending to the flattened empty field now moist with the rains of restoration.

"He sends you abundant showers, both autumn and spring rains as before" (Joel 2:23). After the locust plague, the Lord sent abundant rain to show He'd accepted the changed hearts of the Israelites. The drought would end, and the harvest would return, just as before. But that's not all; the Lord's presence would again be among them. The rain is a sign that the Lord is restoring the alliance between Himself and His people.

"Through all this," Ginger says, "I've asked myself, did I really know the Lord at all? Yes, I was a Christian and very excited at first to believe, but I never took God seriously. I'd never been tested. God really got my attention, didn't He?"

Ginger now categorizes the periods of her life as "B.L." and "A.L."—*Before Locusts* and *After Locusts*.

Do you remember that in the first chapter of this book we discussed how the plagues in the Old Testament were meant to turn the people's hearts back to God? If you don't bolt from this, don't try and run away from your pain, this is the promised outcome: Your heart will be full of God.

Crowding out the fear.

"He seems so much more real to me now, so much closer than ever before," Ginger says. "There's an intimacy now, like one with a partner."

Back in chapter 5, Natalie introduced me to a closer relationship with God: "For your Maker is your husband—the LORD Almighty is his name" (Isa. 54:5). There comes a time in every journey through loss when God calls us back to Him. He's never left us, but sometimes we leave Him, if only briefly. Because our souls are temporarily dark, we don't see His light, and we can't trust and follow His lead. We wonder, is He really going to be there at our side through this?

Though we are the ones who've stepped back and become distant, He longs to draw us close, to bring a blessing to those He loves. "Though the mountains be shaken and the hills be removed, yet my unfailing love for you will not be shaken nor my covenant of peace be removed" (Isa. 54:10).

I am not afraid of storms, for I am learning how to sail my ship.
—Louisa May Alcott

Valerie is experiencing this as God is walking beside her now. I've not met Valerie in person, not yet. She answered my e-mail request for stories about loss telling me, "I have never shared this before, and though I have also written a book, I only hinted at my past but never said what happened. I knew I would someday, but the time just never seemed right. When I read of your topic and the promise of Joel 2:25, I knew the time had come. Whether or not this story is right for your book, it has gone a long way in healing for me just to write it down."

As a child Valerie felt like an ugly misfit, a black goat among white sheep. "I was so tall my brother called me 'totem pole.' My true feelings were deep inside; I was born different, and therefore I must be bad."

Feeling inadequate as a woman, at nineteen she married a boy she didn't even like, desperate for something to give meaning and importance to her life, something to make her feel normal. Two years and two children later, she was divorced and feeling worse than ever about her life.

She started to attend church in hopes of finding answers to her feelings of being "different." She begged, screamed, and pouted, but God was remarkably quiet. "I figured God didn't listen to people like me." The weekends found her in bars living it up or in motels with men she'd just met and would never see again. "The lower my morals became, the more I slept around. I despised me and everything I represented."

Eight years later she remarried for convenience. John needed someone to watch his three children, and Valerie needed someone to pay the bills and let her be a stay-at-home mom. A fair exchange, it seemed. "Life just got worse. Problems with the children; my son was sent to prison. For years I tried to give John what he needed as a husband, but I felt like a prostitute, my body in exchange for family security. I really just wanted to walk away and never come back."

If she wasn't normal, wasn't it God's fault? He'd made her this way. What a cruel joke to play!

"I spent a lot of time going to seminars and ladies' retreats for two reasons—one, to escape my miserable life for awhile, and, the other, to hope for the off chance that I might find out why God disliked me so much."

Nothing made sense until a divine appointment with Florence and Fred Littauer. They were teaching a workshop entitled "Healing the Mind from the Memories That Bind." Her life was transformed, she says, forever changed through this couple. "I walked into the seminar with confusion and shame and walked away with the dawning of understanding. I finally uncovered why I couldn't cope with my own life, why I felt unloved and different from everyone else."

Sexual abuse is not an easy thing to discuss, and Valerie had denied its existence in self-defense. As Fred Littauer worked with her, the pieces and memories began to fall into place, and the truth finally broke through. "I began to feel what I knew was the voice of God speaking to me. I could sense His broad chest as I leaned my head on His shoulder while we walked through the rubble of my life."

Jesus had never abandoned her for a moment. He had been sitting by her side crying the same tears. "I have come to accept that this side of heaven I will not know why this happened to me, but I have come to believe that God will not waste any of my experiences. If I allow Him, He'll use them to help others in similar circumstances. If I can help one person walk away from a life of lingering, pain-filled memories into a world overflowing with freedom through Christ, then my agony of remembering has been worth it."

What about her marriage? Though the years stole what God intended to be the most wonderful expressions of love between a husband and wife, Valerie partnered with God to rouse a stirring in her heart for John. She's working with her Heavenly Father to produce a new crop of passion born from Him, the author of love. "It has not been easy, but this past year has been a time of blending our emotions, our needs, and our love into a more satisfying union."

The couple just celebrated twenty years of marriage, and they have served as missionaries to the Ukraine and Hawaii. "He's done so much for us and our children, and now as a couple. I'm definitely not too old for God to restore the years the locusts devoured. Those painful, lonely, dark years can never be replaced or relived, but the future can be filled with a beauty that God originally intended. I anticipate with great expectation the love God will give us in our future."

When she explained how the Littauers helped her open the wounds of the past, her words reminded me that God never leaves the ground unplowed. Back in the early nineties I attended Advanced CLASS with Florence, eager to get more in-depth training on developing my "someday" speaking and writing ministry. (It was a ways off, but I had optimistic anticipation!)

One morning I rustled around in my tote bag for a pen to take notes during a workshop with Marilyn Heavilyn. Marilyn has lost three precious sons and speaks frequently on the grief process. My eyes still scouring the bottom of the bag, I heard her say that we must allow ourselves to grieve for *every loss,* or we can never be fully whole for the Lord.

Slowly I sat erect, as she spoke straight to my heart. I tried to quell my surging emotion but bolted out of my seat and left the room. I couldn't stop the flow of tears—breathless tears, soak-your-shirt type of tears. *Give it over, Jan,* I felt the Lord say. *Grieve now for your little baby girl.*

But I'm at a writing and speaking seminar!

This is the time and the place.

After I went into premature labor at seven months and delivered my stillborn child, I closed the door on that incident of my life and never mentioned it again. Over the years I blocked out what had happened to me, stuffing the secret deep inside. When medical records forms asked, *"How many pregnancies?"* I'd mark "two" instead of "three."

But my wonderful God knows that secrets are like tooth decay; they start out small and hidden in the crevices, their ache dulled by new jobs, new places, new people. But one day the ache's relentless throbbing will finally force it out.

That morning I saw her face in my mind, my firstborn daughter, and gave way to my grief. I shed tears for the life on earth she didn't get to have and for my shame in feeling relieved of the burden.

Those tears were all part of God's restoration plan. Joel told the people, "God has given you the autumn rains of righteousness" (2:23). Before I could be fully healed, I had to be cleansed. What good is a restored field if it's full of lingering, stubborn weeds? Before the fruits of a whole life could take root, my soul had to be "weed free"—free of guilt, shame, and buried secrets.

Like Valerie, when the time was right and I was ready to face my past, God led me to a seminar where someone else's words unzipped my "hush-hush" file, the hidden panel behind which I held my little secret in safe deposit.

Only it wasn't really safe there.

When we are grounded in truth, the Bible says, "God is our refuge and strength, an ever-present help in trouble" (Ps. 46:1).

I had no intentions of bringing this subject up here in this book. Though I'd grieved and resolved this part of my past, what purpose could it have now? Do readers have to know everything, I asked myself?

But when I jotted down the outline, there it was, listed in bold type: *Stillbirth, Loss of a Child*. Child—the first time I'd seen it in print.

When you walk with God in the fields of your future, He wants nothing to trip you up. No rocks of regret, sharp stones of secrets, no submerged boulders of bitterness.

Hitched to the plow with God. Just picture yourself yoked together with the Lord, side by side, working on your precious soul, and the bonus: you get to know the one you depend on, and to understand Him better and better. If you falter, He will wait, and when you sweat from exhaustion, He'll wipe the beads of moisture from your brow.

Just imagine the new crop He has in mind for you. "Be glad, . . . for he has given you the autumn rains in righteousness" (Joel 2:23). Your field is ready to cultivate. Only He knows how many passes it will take to plow the ground and how much compost to work into the soil. And what is compost, anyway, but a garbage pile? Who can put our past garbage to use better than God, the ultimate conservationist?

On a recent Sunday our pastor said that every miracle in the Bible starts with a problem, a gigantic, over-your-head problem. We usually offer, "This is how you can solve it for me, Lord," as if God is in heaven waiting for suggestions.

We're down here expecting a magic wand to erase the trouble away, but it won't happen. He wants our help to make a miracle.

When the pastor said this, I grabbed my pen: *Without God, you cannot. Without you, God cannot.* (If he only knew how many of his sermon goodies are threaded into this book.)

God will make a miracle; He will bring your harvest in, but not without you. Be prepared for a bit of back strain and roughened hands. Even if you complain, though, He won't threaten to slap you silly, as Scarlett did to her unwilling sister, Suellen in the ruined fields of Tara. "You can't make me work in these fields," Suellen blurted, as Scarlett tossed a gourdful of water at her hot, flushed face.

We won't get doused from the Lord, but one thing is sure: there will be no sitting under the old oak tree sipping iced tea while the Lord toils in our fields.

We don't develop *any* spiritual muscle that way.

My friend, Renee, has more pluck than anyone I know, and she got it spading the soil with her sidekick, Jesus. Abused as a child, she married young as a way of escape from the situation, only to find herself with a husband whose answer to stress was to knock her around and whose anger eventually led him to take his own life. "I guess you could argue that he backed out of life with his finger on the trigger," Renee says.

But he left her a son, William, nicknamed "Bud," a treasured consolation for all the struggle and a joy she thought she would never have. "The doctors said I'd never carry a child because of my autoimmune disease," Renee told me. When she met Ron, a building contractor five years younger, she warned him, "I'm not a good wife candidate. I can't have your children."

He didn't care. They'd have Bud. What more could he want?

When this precious boy came to know Jesus through a youth group, he wouldn't stop hounding his parents until they checked the Lord out for themselves. First Ron turned his life over, then Renee. After high school graduation, Bud joined the United States Air Force and was sent to the Philippines. When he called home needing to hear his parents' voices, he'd often repeat a childhood request, "Mama, tell me a story."

A born storyteller just like her Native American grandfather, Renee wove tales of her heritage that captivated Bud all his life. "Write that one down so I can share it with the guys," Bud would urge. So every month she'd send another installment overseas, contriving more plot and vivid characters to keep the young men intrigued with Native American lore.

Those stories kept her son close.

Then Mt. Pinatubo erupted and decimated the air force base, sending Bud back to duty in California, near Sacramento. He'd been home seven months when he took his motorcycle out for a spin. It was a wooded, curvy road near their mountain home, a road he knew so well. Though it was a brisk, unclouded night, Bud's bike hit a tree head on, killing him instantly.

The clear night evolved into dark shadows of grief as Renee tried to come to terms with losing her son. Through her tears, God spoke to her heart: *Finish the story you started for Bud. Write the book.* How, Lord, she wondered? She had no formal education or writers' classes. So Renee scoured writing books and successful authors to learn the craft. She persevered to complete the novel because, "I'd promised Bud an end to the story, and God promised that He would partner with me."

In the next several years she worked on the story's mystery and suspense, revising the twists and turns. "It kept him so alive in my heart," she says. "I'd imagine his face as he read each chapter. Writing the story healed my heart."

Hitched to the plow—or computer—with God.

She writes with the same energy as she digs in the garden, with a firm grip on her goal. God took her rusted tools, the chipped hoe and the splintered shovel of her past, and replaced them with instruments much stronger and better for the task ahead. "He took the clay of my life and worked along with me to heal my heart, developing me as a person first, then as a writer." Through it all, she entered into a new relationship with the Lord. And Ron felt God's urging to go back to school, to get a degree in divinity, so that he could plant a church in an agricultural community. Renee is now a pastor's wife.

She will never stop missing Bud. "But my novel is so full of him. I love getting up each day and turning on my laptop to see what happens next. I know he's brainstorming with me from heaven." With the novel now submitted to agents and editors, Renee has nearly finished the second book in what will become a trilogy.

Bud had no idea what he started with that simple request, "Mama, tell me a story."

Renee thanks God for an erupted volcano. "It gave me seven sweet months with him I never would have had if a mountain hadn't copped an attitude."

She now says, "I had no idea that Ron and I would ever be in ministry. Not us! And I never would have chosen this way for me, but I'm better off now in my soul than if I'd never encountered any of the locust storms."

Don't just survive, she urges. Live in spite of it. Jesus never set out to find someone to heal. The people He restored always took the first step.

So if you want to partner with God, get your pitchfork and come on down!

CHAPTER FIFTEEN

BRINGING IN THE SHEAVES

I will repay you for the years the locusts have eaten.
—Joel 2:25

"YOU CANNOT HAVE BACK your time," said Charles Spurgeon, "but there is a strange and wonderful way in which God can give back to you the wasted blessings, the unripened fruits of the years over which you have mourned."[1]

After a few trips up and back to the Pacific Northwest, Ginger found her home of new beginnings, a small cottage in Coos Bay, not far from the beach. "I'm going to take a medical assisting course and then get a job. I'm ready now, not afraid anymore. I finally feel confident that I won't end up a bag lady."

Oh, no? That gave me an idea for her going-away party. We'd all come dressed as bag ladies, in the worst old rags we could scrounge. "Oh, come on," Jeanne said, "You can't be serious. Bag ladies? I just bought a new jumpsuit I want to wear."

"We were all down and out before Jesus got a hold on us, weren't we? Humor me with this one."

So we gathered that night, the Bible study group and the prayer breakfast ladies, dressed in some old secondhand finds. We stood in a circle and tossed off the vintage clothing as a symbol of God's renovation power.

Don't you love it that God is in the makeover business?

We put together an Oregon survival kit: stationary and stamps to keep in touch, a phone card just in case she missed us and had no change on hand, and a refrigerator photo magnet of the whole gang at a Neil Diamond concert. I added a fat rubber grasshopper, a prize claimed with a pitiful wad of tickets won at the Ponderosa Ranch shooting gallery near Lake Tahoe.

Previously she had slumped a bit with the loss of hope, but Ginger now stood with posture erect and head high to praise God's name. The nearly broken relationship with Him was now healed.

Suddenly a wave of the weeps splashed over me. Almost a year had passed since I'd first seen this woman pouting into her coffee cup at Sweet Pea's, barely able to utter her prayer needs. A year since the day she walked up my steps for the first cup of tea and conversation, since she first mumbled, "I thought this only happened to other people."

I'd come into her life to encourage her, to make her burden lighter, and to pass on what I'd learned from my own journey. But in the process she had given me something priceless—her pure pain, her undisguised anger, and her unclassified confusion. With them, she offered her trust and an invitation inside her bruised heart. Without knowing me, she let me be a buffer, a temporary shelter where she could grapple with the changes in her life.

She allowed me an orchestra seat for the greatest show on earth—to see God's repayment plan in action.

Right before Peter was martyred, he wrote his second epistle, highlighting God's great and precious promises to people of the faith. "Therefore I will always remind you about these things, even though you know them and are established in the truth you have" (2 Pet. 1:12).

He didn't want the people to forget where the disciples' teaching originated. In verse 16 he says, "We did not follow cleverly contrived myths when we made known to you the power and coming of our Lord Jesus Christ; instead, we were eyewitnesses of His majesty."

Testifiers to His tales.

As we rounded the dining room table to pile our plates high with the potluck, a thought took hold. *Tell the tale.*

Here we were, all lined up together, most of us in various stages of restoration. Oh, not always in the way we had hoped, often in quite another. Each one had her own story, her own version as an eyewitness to His majesty.

And for our sorrow, the Lord repaid us with interest.

I looked at Jeanne with the twinkle in her eye as she planned a summer as a mission builder with Youth with a Mission, Connie still enchanted with her new motherhood, Nadine just beginning to date Mark, Claudia with a new job as head nurse at the California Legislature and a cofounder of a singles ministry. And Mary Gail, Julie, and me, along with the prayer breakfast gals: Della, Carol, Kathryn.

Yes, our stories could tell a tale. But when? How? Serious writing, with my busy life? I had my job at the Capitol and a very long commute; my daughters were still quite the challenge; and our Saturday night singles ministry demanded a lot of my time.

Plus, I had written nothing more than newsletters and silly skits for years. A book? Far too complicated a project.

But I remembered the words from Habakkuk. Yes, there is always a tip from the prophets of old when you need one.

God told Habakkuk that He was going to do something he wouldn't believe, and then He told the prophet to "write down the revelation and make it plain on tablets" (Hab. 2:2).

So I jotted some notes and tucked the idea away in my file cabinet along with Ginger's new address in Oregon.

How I would miss that copper-haired beauty!

Saying goodbye to Ginger proved a defining moment in my life, for it signified my true understanding of the eternal perspective—being less concerned for what we lose than with how the losses can impact someone else.

There would be new vistas looming wide in front of me and more Gingers out there desperate to understand God's provisions and the promise of Joel 2:25.

Our singles group mushroomed in the next few years. We went from a handful gathered in a living room to over seventy who met at the "King's Place," an office-building-turned-church that one of our members let us use at no charge. We met on Saturday nights to praise the Lord, to get to know other singles, and to grow in our faith.

Jeanne and I hummed with excitement as we planned meetings and events with our ministry team. We barely thought about our dateless existence. (Notice I said "barely.") We put our own yen for a godly marriage on the back burner as God filled our pot to overflowing with opportunities to serve.

Like all singles groups, people came and went through the revolving door of fellowship. We saw lives change through healthy connections, and we learned from excellent speakers who shared wisdom with us on everything from spiritual gifts to sexuality.

Every teacher needs to keep ahead of the students, and because other singles continually approached us for relationship advice (if you're up front every week, others assume that you are well-informed on the issues), our team made the seminar rounds, soaking up everything possible on being a whole person, dating, and remarriage.

If we knew nothing else, it was that these choices affect your whole life.

I read every book conceivable on the subject. Where had these guidebooks been when I heard all those sweet nothings whispered in my ear? That was yesterday. I was reaching out to my future.

One summer night our group had a western barbecue and hoedown and presented a play featuring a Southern belle

(Jeanne) searching for her true love. I played the fairy god-mother who sauntered in like Mae West and hurled advice.

When Carl first saw me, I was on stage in a baby pink cow-girl dress with yards of fringe, flailing my magic rope wand. He thought to himself, "Here is an interesting woman. She could be fun."

Over the next months we bumped into each other every-where, and my heart sang a chorus of "This Could Be the Start of Something Good." It wasn't just his premature silver hair or his steel blue eyes but his strength of character. Here was a man who had stayed faithful to his first marriage, who didn't choose to end it, a man who sought God's wisdom in his life—a man I could trust.

Every time we talked, I felt like a soggy piece of toast. But each time I gazed longingly into his eyes, there were merely congenial smiles in return.

"He guards his heart like he's the sentry of the crown jewels," I huffed to Jeanne. I took a deep breath. "What is the matter with me? I am a mature, professional woman, not a schoolgirl dizzy with her first crush. This is ridiculous," I told myself.

"You're in love with the idea of falling in love," she advised. "He's fresh out of a marriage, and he needs to be sin-gle for a while. The timing just isn't right."

I nodded at her counsel. By now I had learned the wisdom of the right timing.

There are no disappointments to those whose wills
are buried in the will of God.
—Frederick Faer

In the next two years we grew in a friendship, and Carl had a few dates, but none with me. That old bantering kept buzzing in my ear. Rejected. Not good enough. Loser.

No! I slapped myself at the thought. I had come too far to buy that nonsense. The question I had to ask myself was, Do I care about this man enough to want the best for him, even if it will never be me?

My answer brought a new lesson on an old truth: love is putting another's good ahead of your own. Love truly is letting go.

So I did. A year later Carl called me on the off chance I'd be available as his date for a company bowling party. And so it began, a year of testing—learning God's character, of developing our trust, and of discovering God's design for a marriage that would glorify Him.

Concepts a bit foreign to me in my previous life.

I determined to stick to my holy fast, and Carl made it easy; he became the moral leader in our dating, determined to do it God's way or no way at all.

If only I could find a man for Jeanne so we could transition into married-ness together. *How about it, Lord? Can you bring someone for her?* No candidates emerged, but she joined in my happiness, relishing every detail of my courtship and helping to plan the wedding.

We never mentioned splitting up the team. Though Jeanne's personality still sparkled, I could sense the underlying pain as she prepared herself to go solo without me. Hadn't I been in the same place with Natalie, watching her go off over the rainbow and wondering what lay ahead for me?

Like Siamese twins we faced the dividing of our joined selves, uncertain how our friendship would need to change. Later we stole a few private moments together.

"It's bittersweet for me," I confessed. I could not enter this life with Carl without a twinge of sadness at the changes. She wouldn't be popping over in her pajamas anymore, or calling me at five in the morning to ask me to pray about something, or leaving me a message, "Set up the Scrabble board. It's payback time."

How odd that the season of my life I had fiercely resisted (because it was forced on me) was now so cherished because of this dear friendship!

On my wedding eve in 1995, after writing my vows, I penned a letter to Jeanne. Tears flowed again as I recounted all our antics together, how she buoyed me up with her cheerfulness, and how she will always have a special place in my heart:

> You stood firm and trusted in the Lord when your dreams were ruined, and your strength and optimism was something I longed to embrace. With you as my buddy, I never laughed so much, and my gloomy days became shorter and shorter.
>
> Thank you for inspiring me to be the best, for living life with gusto, no matter what, for loving me despite my quirks. I knew if I ever got married again, it would be because God prepared me through the test of our friendship. You will always be my "sis" and will have a place in my heart that no one else can ever share.

She stood next to me when we exchanged our vows, and I gave her a quick wink when Carl said, "Thank you for waiting for me, Jan. I had to become the man you needed me to be."

Life can be like a fairy tale if we let God write the story.

My Heavenly Father walked me down the aisle and gave me in marriage to a man who would enhance my life for His purposes, not my own.

God did not bring me another husband until He had restored me to wholeness. The Bible says that a broken cistern cannot hold water.

When Joel finally tells the people that God will remove their affliction (Joel 2:25), it's because they've returned to Him with their broken hearts, with their sincere prayers of faith. They had suffered enough and had learned some pretty stiff lessons, but the Lord wants to make up for all the damage the locusts had done and to compensate for the loss, the famine, the drought, the waste.

What started as devastation and sorrow ends with joy and abundance.

Proverbs 24:27 counsels us to complete our plowing: "Finish your outdoor work and get your fields ready; after that, build your house."

Once the plowing in our hearts is completed, it will be time to build toward the future. If we do the tough work—the plowing, first—we won't be erecting our dreams on sand dunes, constructing our hopes with matchsticks, or depending on a house of cards that can tip over with the slightest nudge.

That gives me a basketful of comfort. How about you?

Know this: Your loving Savior has your best in mind; He's had it from the very beginning.

There are times when I shake my head in wonder at the strange and wonderful way He has redeemed my lost years, my ruined dreams. The way He has brought new opportunities, unexpected friends, and adventures unimaginable. And how I've come to the place of wanting not only God's blessings but also God Himself.

My spirit has found a joyous peace, a wholeness, a harmony—*after the locusts.*

CHAPTER SIXTEEN

TOOT YOUR HORN OF PLENTY

And you will praise the name of the Lord your God,
who has worked wonders for you.

—Joel 2:26

JOEL EXPLAINS GOD'S ACTIONS as "wonders," things that can't be explained in any other way. Only the Lord could have sent in the locusts and then banished them, events that caused some wide eyes, some rattled brains, and some huge U-turns in people's lives.

After my daughter Jennifer's accident, I had no choice but to take a leave from work to help out with her young boys while she recovered. Carl suggested I simply resign from the senator's office. "You've been wrestling with this yen to write full-time for over a year now," he said. "This looks like God's timing to me. When Jenny is well, you should begin your writing career, start fulfilling your dreams."

Yikes! Leave my security, my identity? Risk the unknown? "We only go around this life once," Carl reminded me, without saying, *You're not getting any younger, you know.*

Not only did God bring Jenny back to wellness from a severe brain injury, but also He used the accident to jolt me into my passion. Just like with the people in Joel's time, He used disaster to stir me to a new sense of His will.

Without Carl, I may not have been so courageous, but with his gentle hand in the middle of my back, I said good-bye to California politics, and hello to submissions, rejections, revisions and a loud "Yee haw!" when I saw my byline.

It was for *Miracle in the Rain,* the story of Jenny's accident, published in *Virtue Magazine* in 1999. My story focused not on the amazing rescue but the miracle God performed in our hearts, mine and Jenny's, through the ordeal.

And on the lesson: we need constantly to remember that God always has a purpose for our problems.

With this story, my first ever in a Christian publication, God reminded me that He always salvages our pain and refashions it to profit others. He will take the worst that ever happens to us and sift it thoroughly to reveal the priceless nuggets.

We live in the California Gold Rush country, our rolling hills the source of the most extraordinary human stampede the world has ever known. Have you ever tried to pan for gold? After a minute of whirling a pan in the hopes of separating a speck of heavy gold from the useless sand, I get bored with the slow process and begin thinking of finding a sarsaparilla to quench my thirst.

Imagine, even on a good day those forty-niners could only wash about fifty pans from a stream. Once they dried the flecks, the men would cautiously fill their pouches and cleverly hide them around their tents until the opportunity to trek to the assay office. No loot-hungry losers would dare steal their stash!

Isn't it wonderful that our God doesn't hide His wealth? That He is into joint possession?

The area where I live is also called the mother lode, named for the rich vein of gold that ribboned through the hills, where the winter snow melt washed the glittery metal into rivers and streams for the adventurers to find. We are God's mother lode, His root of treasure, His horn of plenty. And He is the King of the gold panners. Can't you see Him, gliding that pan full of wet soot that we are, spiraling it with His agile hands, ever so gently so as not to lose a single speck of gold, only the grit that keeps us from gleaming?

And where do these specks usually end up? Melted down to be purified. Otherwise, the gold is dull and devalued. The purer the gold, the pricier it is.

You've been through some sort of fire, haven't you? It has scorched your heart and burned your faith. And your battle has not been just to believe but to keep on believing in the promises while God cranks up the heat.

Malachi said it well: "For he will be like a refiner's fire . . . He will . . . refine them like gold and silver" (Mal. 3:3).

While He cleans, the Lord also clarifies. As God skims, so goes the scum. And we become more the people He intends us to be. Once we embrace this truth, it's simply impossible not to share it with others.

After Joel delivers his pleas for repentance in the second chapter, God Himself speaks to the people, assuring them of repayment for the locust years and promising them, "You will have plenty to eat, until you are full, and you will praise the name of the LORD your God, who has worked wonders for you" (Joel 2:26).

Ask my friend, Kathy, about wonders. She takes every opportunity to proclaim the work God did in her life. Tall and slim, with flashing blue eyes, she radiates warmth and compassion now, but years ago she was an angry, abusive mother, a perfectionist with impossible expectations for her family. Though she'd been a longtime Christian, she couldn't grasp God's strength to help her control herself.

She had to walk through some fire to get things right, to learn how to choose His joy, and to realize that people didn't hold the key to happiness; the Lord did.

"I did improve slowly," she said, "but I tended to discount any progress made if it wasn't a 100 percent improvement. I couldn't give credit or praise to others if they didn't fulfill my desires completely."

During her healing time, Kathy began to feel God patiently working with her. "Suddenly it made sense. I kept focusing on what I hadn't done right rather than giving God praise for what He had accomplished in me. I would condemn myself for the 10 percent I hadn't done well, even if I'd grown 90 percent in another area.

"It changed everything," she says. "God is faithful. He replaced my anger with joy, rebuilt my love for my children, and renewed the love between Larry and me."

She blesses others through her writing, and she and Larry speak at seminars and retreats about how God restored many wasted years.

Unafraid of making herself vulnerable, Kathy speaks candidly about the past. "There is nothing like truth to reach into the heart and open people to the healing hope in the Lord Jesus," she says.

Truth consists of having the same idea
about something that God does.
—Joseph Joubert

Anne is learning to share the wonders God has brought to her. After a failed marriage, decades of depression, illness, and financial struggle, she toiled on life's treadmill. It took all her might just to make it through another day.

In the early 1990s she wandered into our singles group to find direction, and as He always does, God aimed her straight into His Word. It didn't hurt that she started hanging out with us, a group of bachelor girls always singing "Someday My Prince Will Come" in optimistic anticipation of our time in eternity with Jesus.

When I shared the promise in Joel, it sparked a momentary hope that would flicker with each financial or medical setback.

"Press into Him," Jeanne would tell her. "Just trust, and He'll come through in a big way, you watch."

She'd smile faintly and nod. She didn't expect much more from her silver platter than tarnish.

In her late forties by this time, working three jobs to survive, Anne was weary. We always tried to cheer her up, and one weekend she was able to sneak away up to the cabin with us. One night we hunched together in our beach chairs around the fire pit, preparing our sticks and marshmallows for a s'mores pigout. Rolling my white puff around the sheets of flame, I remarked in mock seriousness, "You know, in some cultures they eat locusts."

Claudia murmured, "Oh, get out of here."

"Seriously, the Bible says John the Baptist dined on them frequently. Look it up! They're a delicacy in some cultures. Cambodians stuff peanuts inside and fry them in a wok. In Botswana, they skewer and barbecue them until golden brown.'"

"Yuk!" was the resounding echo.

"Crunchy and dried, they might be good for dipping in salsa. A real Tex-Mex treat," I tossed out.

"Frankly," Mary Gail stated with a sober face, "the only way to enjoy them is honey roasted."

Jeanne chuckled and got into the swing of it. "As for me, I'll take mine dipped in chocolate. Chocolate-covered critters, we could market those at the street fair in Old Town."

"Absolutely," I piped. "And I have a great idea. A recipe book for bug banquets. The possibilities are endless: caramel critters, locust licks."

"Don't forget fruity fondue," Connie added, "for the diet-conscious."

We were howling in laughter at our absurdity, when suddenly Anne flung her messy marshmallow stick to the ground. "What's that big black thing? It's moving!"

An overstuffed wood beetle slogged through her dessert, striking out with all eight legs to free himself from the gushy goo. Before we could sing "Kumbaya my Lord," he was a bug bonfire. When we got into our sleeping bags that night, we were still cackling about it.

From then on, Anne really took things a bit lighter. She agreed with us that if we can laugh at it, we can live with it. We can not only survive the locusts; we can feast on them too.

A year or so later, she sat in Jeanne's living room and quietly shared, "I got a surprise call this week. From the child I placed for adoption, over thirty years ago." Anne's daughter, born before she and her former husband were married, wanted to get acquainted with her birth mother.

Stunned and scared, she needed prayer for the upcoming meeting.

"What a marvelous girl she is," Anne told us later with a tear twinkling in her eye. "I've struggled with so much guilt and regret over this. And now she wants to be close with me. She's thrilled to know her two brothers." Instantly the two women bonded.

This proved only the beginning of God's repayment plan. Not too long after, she met a man who adored her style of deep, profound thinking. "And he makes me laugh!" she said. A year later they were married on Valentine's Day.

We were the ones with the smirk on our faces. "Told you, oh ye of little faith!"

Anne is slowly introducing her daughter to the entire family. There are still relatives left to include, and she is trying to be delicate about breaking the news. Soon everyone will know the secret of her past that has now become the joy of her future.

She says, "I'm anxious to tell the world what God has done." And to toot her horn of plenty.

To live in the hearts we leave behind is not to die.
                                            —Thomas Campbell

Last year our pastor and his wife lost their five-year-old daughter to a brain tumor. Phyllis and her husband Norm, also familiar with losing a child, helped start a grief-support ministry at our church. That's how I got to know them and their story.

The doctors told Phyllis she would never have children, but she and Norm rejoiced with the miracle when Phyllis became pregnant. Lori was the delight of their life—a good student, a competitive swimmer, a tennis player, and a model daughter who loved the Lord. One night, twenty years ago, came a tragic call from the state trooper's office. While driving home for summer break from college, their beloved daughter had fallen asleep at the wheel and had been killed when the car rolled over.

"Lord, it can't be Lori," Phyllis blurted. "She's our only child. I just know you'd never take her away from us. God, why? What good could possibly come from something so awful?"

"The next year was the most difficult of my life," Phyllis told me. "Yet in some ways I would actually grow to cherish that painful, poignant, heartbreaking year more than any other time I have known. It became a time of growing close to the Lord. The most important thing I've learned since Lori's death is that there is life—not just existence, but a rich, joy-filled life, even after something so senseless and tragic as losing a child."

She's discovered a new horizon in the aftermath of tragedy, as Lori's presence filled her life. "I don't mean she was present in any supernatural way but rather in very simple and real ways. I'd know just what she'd say if she could be here, things like, 'I know you miss me, Mom, but you don't do me any favors by being depressed. You still have a life to live.'"

Less than a year after losing Lori, their pastor called. Would they visit a couple in their church whose sons were killed? Phyllis and Norm ended up in a Bible study with three other couples who had also lost children, and one Mother's Day they all drove to up the California coast to Mendocino. "We had services by the ocean, sitting on blankets," Phyllis said. "We simply shared about the children we had lost."

Reaching out to others and telling them how God worked wonders for her helped Phyllis regain happiness and meaning in her life. In the two decades since Lori's death, Phyllis has made herself available to hundreds of grief-stricken people. "It seemed that whenever a couple lost a child anywhere in our valley, our phone would ring. Many times we'd be at the couple's side within an hour or two, helping them cope with the initial shock of their loss."

Phyllis often takes women on retreats, speaks to churches and community groups, and gives mini-workshops on grief. Not a trained counselor or speaker, Phyllis is just an ordinary woman with simple words about rediscovering the joy of living. "It actually petrifies me to speak in front of a crowd," she admits, "but God gives me the strength. He has allowed me to see my sorrow and brokenness rewoven into healing and benefit for others, and He can do the same for anyone who is open to it."

Phyllis knows that if Lori could come back to earth and observe how things are now, she'd be happy about it. "Her dad and I are living a life that is honoring to her memory."

Back in Joel's day, the people recognized God in their midst because of the wonders, the restorative miracles, that He performed.

Why? So they could have full tummies and fatter pocket-books? No, for the spiritual blessings, so the people would praise His name and claim His promises.

For generations to come.

There is a need for healing in our country today, in our families, and in our hearts. People are broken, hurting, and lost in a world with no real answers for their pain. If you've experienced a wonder from the Lord, in the form of a remolded life or a renewed dream, He'll make good use of it.

The transformation of grief into ministry, Phyllis says, is the ultimate form of healing for the hurt of loss.

CHAPTER SEVENTEEN

FAITH INTO FACT

I will pour out my spirit on all people.
—Joel 2:28

JOEL HAD ANOTHER PROMISE for Israel's future at the end of this second chapter—the Holy Spirit would be poured out in great abundance over everyone who believed. If we study the verses closely, we see that he's talking about the earth's end times, when the Lord will judge the nations. But for His special ones, those who've seen His miracles in our lives, who trust in Him, we will have no reason to fear.

After the locusts, how many would dare say that God was not in control?

If you trace back in the Old Testament, you'll see how many of Israel's heroes found invisible power when God gave them enormous challenges. Suddenly they had energy that defied all odds.

Guess what? God promises us that energy, too, through the Holy Spirit, the life force of all who call Jesus Lord. When the turbulence bashes us around, the Spirit gives us the stamina to endure. It's the Spirit's power that sweeps into our lives to salvage us from the wreckage.

Terri's hurricane came suddenly, but she can attest to the might of the Spirit that sustained her. In 1980 her husband was in a freak motorcycle accident. A semi-truck plunged off an overpass to the freeway below, and in ditching the bike to save himself, Bob broke his neck. He is now a quadriplegic.

When the facts sunk in, the truth of what life was going to be like for this family with three young preschoolers, Terri dreaded each day and cowered in her heart from what lay ahead. "It was overwhelming. I knew I couldn't handle it, but I had to," she told me.

Days were excruciatingly lonely. Although people came forward to help in wondrous ways, Terri still felt isolated. "I wondered if God saw or heard my prayers. I knew He did, intellectually, but I didn't always feel it. I felt He had deserted us. I couldn't see what good could possibly come out of this situation."

And how could she ever measure up to the "proper" godly attitudes and the "right spirit" of surrender to her circumstances?

Terri and the family stumbled through many changes. It wasn't only the issue of a paralyzed husband and life with ramps and continual care; there were the financial pressures, the leadership in the home, and the psychological aftermath for all of them, especially Bob.

Exhausted, she had no other choice but to keep going.

"I died to my dreams so many times, for many years," she says. "Step by step, week by week, year by year, I had to relinquish expectations and accept the fact that life would never be normal for any of us."

A few years later, though bruised and broken inside, Terri knew she had a choice to make—either to become bitter or become better. "I really wanted God on my side, so I made conscious choices, though sometimes whimperingly, to let God be God and let Him be my refuge."

She found amazing power to endure when she came to the feet of Jesus. "As I sit and listen to Him and talk to Him and cry with Him, I get to know Him better."

"Satan had lied to me about the severity of God. God wasn't the villain; he wasn't picking on me because I was one of His bad children. Seeing it from that perspective suddenly changed everything—not the circumstances, of course—but me."

Just about this time a financial settlement came through. "A generous settlement," she says gratefully. "The Lord has been faithful to all five of us. We're OK with what is familiar and comfortable for us. He did, indeed, put a hedge around us and has kept us from many onslaughts that could have brought us down. What Satan meant for evil, God is working for good."

In what specific ways did God replant her ruined dreams, I asked Terri? Her answer came swiftly. "The character he has built into my children. They are strong in their faith because they have witnessed many good things that came from the hand of God." Young adults in their twenties now, "they are the primary fruit in my life," she says.

More eyewitnesses to His majesty and to the truth in Joel 2:27, *"That I am the LORD your God, and that there is no other."*

For eight years, Terri has been a Bible study leader, having a generous measure of influence over hundreds of ladies. Can you see why they can't miss God's infinite grace played out in her life?

"I have a host of friendships I would not have had, had it not been for the accident and how it affected so many people," she adds. "My friendships are deeper and more meaningful now. My knowledge of God and the way He works is so much greater because I am forced to cling to Him."

Terri has reached a place of peaceful acceptance. "It's much better than floundering around asking why and why not all the time."

Terri wrote her story for a Christian woman's magazine several years ago and let me read it when we met in New

Orleans last summer. We sat during lunch with chattering teeth as arctic-like cold air blasted through the air-conditioning vents, but I hardly noticed through our warm conversation. How obvious to me that the Spirit had been poured out in her, and the God of all comfort is her joy.

That night after our meetings, I curled up in my hotel bed to read Terri's story. At one point in the article, Terri explains, "Difficult as I found yielding, with each cry of surrender, my aching heart would declare, 'OK Lord, I accept your will for me today. I'm weak. I'm grasping hold of your strength.'"

Reading the story is one thing; knowing the author is another. Terri has so much to pass on from her painful journey. When I asked, she agreed on the spot. And this is her personal nugget just for you: "Let Him hold your tears in a bottle and be your refuge. Let Scripture, especially the Psalms, Isaiah, and Job become a part of your way of thinking and relating to God."

She practices this as she depends on Him daily, and daily her strength is renewed.

A promise delivered.

He's got big plans for you, too. Just remember this: God rarely restores the years in the same way they were lived, and rarely do we get back the same dreams we lost.

Though Terri's dream of a fairy-tale marriage was destroyed, other dreams have taken their place. God has graciously brought Bob far beyond medical expectations, and today he feeds himself and drives a custom-made van.

Remember her whenever you read this verse, her favorite: "The rock of my strength, my refuge is in God. Pour out your heart before Him; God is a refuge for us" (Ps. 62:7–8 NASB).

The future is so bright it burns your eyes.
—Oprah Winfrey

The summer after we married, Carl and I bought backpacks and two train passes and trekked around Europe like college students. Susan, the widow whose story I related in chapter 6, was eager to house-sit for a month. In part, she wanted to visit Jeanne, but she had also found herself suddenly homeless. Jeanne had spent the previous summer in the mission-builder program with Youth for a Mission in Hawaii and suggested to Susan that she check out doing the same since she had no other responsibilities at the moment.

Why not? Susan had nowhere else to go, and after a few phone calls, she discovered that the YWAM base in San Francisco had an opening. They would be thrilled to have the extra help. (Room and board for another month!)

After we came home from overseas, Susan worked at the YWAM base near Union Square in the City by the Bay. "It was ironic to be now ministering to the homeless—considering that I was one," she says with a chuckle. In one of the craziest cities in the country, she felt strangely calm.

"In ministering to the needy, God was ministering to me."

She and YWAM hit it off marvelously. If only she could find a way to attend the YWAM three-month training (personal study and emotional healing) and follow-up outreach, she thought. Such a prayer seemed impossible.

Then just before her month was up, Susan's father passed away after a long illness, and she rushed down to her small hometown near Bakersfield. After the funeral, Susan's sisters had a surprise for her.

The house with no mortgage belonged to her now.

She also received $5,000 cash. "Exactly what I needed for the Crossroads School!" Off she went to the YWAM base in Texas.

"Those five months were major healing for me," Susan told me. "God was fulfilling his promise of using the bruised reed, showing me He was not passing me by at all; He did have something for me after all."

And if that wasn't enough, after eight years her estranged son finally came home. "He was a broken man, ready to turn his life around, to start anew. Last year he graduated from college. God healed his mind and emotions completely."

Wait a minute—that's not all. Her relationship with her daughters has also been restored. "Like Miriam in the Bible, he turned my mourning into dancing," she says.

It's a bumper crop, wouldn't you say? It's as if the Lord says, "Here it is, I'm paying you back for all you've invested in pain and sorrow and loss. I'll fill you up until you are running over. See, I had it in mind all the time. It's the reward for standing firm and trusting in me. For not abandoning your field and running after a mirage when all appeared to be a total loss."

Joy is sorrow inside out; grief remade again.
—Hannah Hurnard

After Ginger settled in Oregon, she joined a singles group. "It wasn't for me," she admits. "I found a wonderful church and found a best friend who had been through a similar situation of losing a marriage." No longer striving for her own way, Ginger committed herself, simply, to God's way. "In that I found complete peace."

She enrolled in a course geared toward displaced women who lacked confidence. "We all struggled together," she says. "It was such a time of self-discovery." She took a temporary position with the Department of Fish and Wildlife for two years, and one of the fish biologists in her office asked if she'd be interested in meeting his brother sometime. She nodded casually, might be nice, *sometime.* "Then one morning Larry came into the office when I was talking to some customers. He came over, took my hand and introduced himself, asking if I'd like to go to dinner and a movie on Friday night."

It didn't take long for her to see what a wonderful man had asked her out. After a few months the relationship blossomed. "I thought about you," she told me, "and all your 'take it slow' advice. I tried, honestly! You'd have been proud of me."

During their dating time, Ginger developed an awful pain in her eyeball and went blind in one eye for a month. "I felt like damaged goods, depressed and very scared, frantic and in so much pain. After my CT Scan and MRI, I asked Larry what he would do if I had a brain tumor. Do you know what he said? 'We'll just have to get married sooner!' What a guy. There aren't many men around like him." The tests turned out negative, a case of optical neuritis, with no explanation of the cause.

Before her wedding, Ginger called me with the details, her voice brimming with delight. "He's such a sweetie," she said. "I thank the Lord for His grace and mercy to me."

Ginger chose to love again, despite the risk of more loss. "I know now that we grow through loss," she said.

Joy is the echo of God's life within us.
—Joseph Marmion

What does the future hold for you? Who can know? But God is surely in it—that, we do know.

If you've related to any of the stories in this book, you'll know this: If you partner with God, if you let Him restore you for His purposes, whatever darkness you are walking through right now is only for a season.

The other day Jeanne gave me a pamphlet on prayer, and it said, "Pray the promises, not the problems." Pondering that, I see great wisdom. Instead of asking God to remove the problems, ask Him to reveal His promises. Trust Him to keep His word even when it seems impossible, even when the circumstances point in the other direction.

The Book of Joel starts out by getting everybody's attention, using their current crisis as a background for his message. He asks, "Has anything like this ever happened in your days?"

I think not.

It ends with an affirmation: "The LORD dwells in Zion!" (Joel 3:21). Look beyond the circumstances. Believe His promises!

As you close this book, you may still have questions and fears and you may still be hurting, but hopefully you are also propped up with the greatest promise for restoration I've ever found: *God will restore you; He will repay you for the years the locusts have eaten.*

Let your faith believe it. Let your faith become fact.

"At the moments when the future is completely obscured," writes Catherine Marshall, "can any one of us afford to go to meet our tomorrows with dragging feet? God had been in the past. He would be in the future, too."[2]

Just look at the women you've read about. They would say this to you if you were having coffee with them: Dare to go farther with God than your eyes can see. He will lead you where you're hesitant to walk and stay right with you as you work the raw soil of your sorrow together.

Only God can fulfill this promise to take the remnants of your ruined dreams, the residue of your wasted years, and to transform them into a bumper crop that will more than compensate for everything you've lost.

It's a sure thing. If He's your Lord, you've got His spiritual IOU.

Someday you'll be rejoicing, "O LORD, you took up my case; you redeemed my life" (Lam. 3:58). Oh, how I wish I could be around to rejoice with you!

Just get ready to reap. You're in for a harvest that can never be destroyed.

EPILOGUE

AFTER I SENT THE BOOK OFF TO THE PUBLISHER, Carl suggested we take a long-awaited trip to Ireland. The landscape captivated me—the lush, hilly pastures full of sheep and cattle, farm plots divided by stones piled into fences. Landscape that was once entirely useless, where nothing would grow. But diligent and hopeful farmers hauled sand and seaweed up from the shore, layered it on the clay soil, and in time the land was enriched and nourished. Grass now grows abundantly.

While snapping photos of contented sheep in these fields, it struck me: *This is the essence of my book—reclaiming what was once ruined and wasted and restoring it to abundance.*

While I write, our country is in turmoil. As people search for healing, it helps to remember Joel, who pointed out to a confused and fearful nation that God is in control of disaster. Nothing can happen that He will not use for good.

Joel never tried to explain *why* disaster arrived. There's not much comfort in *why*, mostly wrinkles and migraines. But as we examine *the how*, healing begins. If we find the courage to work alongside God, the flawed fields will produce again. We will be like the hardy turf in the Emerald Isle, completely reclaimed. And the result worth every hour and every ounce of sweat and toil.

Let's look again at God's plan for restoration in the Book of Joel. First we must "spend the night in sackcloth" (1:13) and be authentic in our sorrow, for this marks the turning point.

Then comes emotional spring cleaning as we "declare a holy fast" (1:14), letting go of any bitterness, anger at God (even just a bit), any attitude or behavior lurking about ready to sabotage our "whole-life life."

Now it's time to "cry out to the Lord" (1:19) to restore us in whatever way He decides. Admit that nothing can salvage the situation except God Himself. Be willing to stick it out no matter how long it takes or what you must endure.

Next, "Return to the LORD your God with all your heart" (2:13). He is gracious and compassionate and responds in love, even when we don't deserve it.

Recall the women's stories in these pages and take to heart that "He has done great things" (2:21). He is eager to do even more. "Be glad and rejoice" (2:23). Smile with optimistic anticipation. Act *as if* the sunshine of blessing is already shining.

When we're hitched to the plow with God, we move together in the same direction, at the same pace. Let go of the reins, trust your new partner, and the autumn rains of righteousness will come (2:23). The vats will overflow with new wine and oil (2:24).

What began in disappointment and darkness will end in joy and spiritual plenty (2:25). It's a transforming promise with your name engraved on it.

As you look back with a new heart and perspective, you'll be gushing with praises for the Lord who worked incredible wonders for you (2:26).

TO CONTACT AUTHOR

Contact Jan by E-mail at jwriter@foothill.net.
For speaking engagements, check her
Web site at jancoleman.com.

END NOTES

Chapter Two
1. Ruth Bell Graham, *Ruth Bell Graham's Collected Poems* (Grand Rapids: Baker Books, 1997), 262.
2. Eugenia Price, *No Pat Answers* (Garden City, NY: Doubleday), 127.
3. Tim Hansel, *You Gotta Keep Dancin'* (Elgin, IL: David C. Cook, 1985).

Chapter Five
1. Kay Arthur, *As Silver Refined* (Sisters, OR: Waterbrook, 1997), 15.
2. Oswald Chambers, *My Utmost for His Highest* (Grand Rapids: Discovery House, 1992), February 14.

Chapter Six
1. Oswald Chambers, *My Utmost for His Highest*, July 8.

Chapter Seven
1. Liz Curtis Higgs, *Bad Girls of the Bible* (Sisters, OR: Waterbrook, 1999), 8.
2. Florence Litauer, *Silver Boxes: The Gift of Encouragement* (Dallas: Word, 1989), 5–6.

Chapter Eight
1. Linda Shepherd Evans, *Faith Never Shrinks in Hot Water* (Nampa, ID: Pacific Press, 1996). Also quotes from her Web site: www.sheppro.com.

Chapter Eleven
1. Gerald Sittser, *A Grace Disguised* (Grand Rapids: Zondervan, 1995), 97,120.
2. Ibid., 180.

Chapter Fourteen
1. Chambers, *My Utmost for His Highest*, March 8.

Chapter Fifteen
1. Charles Spurgeon quoted in Warren Wiersbe, *Be Amazed* (Colorado Springs: Chariot Victor Publishing, 1996), 57.

Chapter Seventeen
1. Terri Orr Geary, "A Turning Point," *Today's Christian Woman*, November 1989.
2. Catherine Marshall, *To Live Again* (New York: McGraw-Hill, 1957), 332.